"*Teaching Eagles To Soar* is a book I will always keep on my desk for quick reference. I pick it up often in my school day, to help me form thoughts about a subject or topic that I might be discussing with a student or even a teacher. Years of wisdom are contained in the pages of this book. I wish I had had this book years ago."

—Deborah Goforth
Author of *Scars of Love, Tears of Hope*

"*Teaching Eagles To Soar* is perhaps the one book our country needs to help boys and girls who long to find real meaning in life."

—Dr. Gene Hood
President, National Home Life & Accident Insurance Co.

"This book prepares students to become husbands, wives, parents, and citizens. What could be more important? This is a marvelous book."

—John R. Erickson
Author of *Hank the Cow Dog*

"*Teaching Eagles To Soar* is a refreshing book. It is amazing to consider what this world could be like if people truly followed these laws. This book inspires me to live a life of piety."

—Kenneth Kavanaugh
Director of Diamond J. Youth Ranch

"This book provides the foundational principles youth need to build character and solve problems. It provides guidance that many kids never received at home, school or in their neighborhood."

—Duan Hanks
Ex-wide receiver for the Miami Dolphins and Founder/
Director of Incentives Ranch of Texas

TEACHING EAGLES
TO SOAR

TEACHING EAGLES
TO SOAR

Guidance and counseling for a fatherless generation

RONALD E. JOHNSON, C. PH.D

TATE PUBLISHING *& Enterprises*

Published by Tate Publishing & Enterprises, LLC
127 E. Trade Center Terrace | Mustang, Oklahoma 73064 USA
1.888.361.9473 | www.tatepublishing.com

Tate Publishing is committed to excellence in the publishing industry. The company reflects the philosophy established by the founders, based on Psalm 68:11,
"The Lord gave the word and great was the company of those who published it."

Book design copyright © 2009 by Tate Publishing, LLC. All rights reserved.
Cover design by Leah LeFlore
Interior design by Stephanie Woloszyn

Published in the United States of America

ISBN: 978-1-60799-256-1
1. Education/Counseling   2. General
09.04.13

TABLE OF CONTENTS

ACKNOWLEDGEMENTS

To Nancy Johnson, my beloved wife, whose insights, inspiration and encouragement kept me focused on completion of this book.

To the teenagers who shared their stories and asked questions from which grew *Teaching Eagles to Soar.*

To Sarah Barbee who transcribed my notes into an organized manuscript.

To Lydia Seals whose illustrations brought clarity to the manuscript.

To David Wilson who labored persistently to put the book in format for publication.

To the team at Tate Publishing Company for guiding me through the process of turning a manuscript into an attractive and meaningful book.

" ... they shall mount up with wings as eagles; they shall run and not be weary, they shall walk and not faint."

—Isaiah 40:31

INTRODUCTION

Teaching Eagles to Soar grew out of more than 45 years as an educator of youth, conference speaker, and teacher of educators in both the public and private sectors. Throughout those decades, similar behavior patterns, catastrophes and successes among youth were evident.

Tragically, the increasing condition of father-challenged homes has resulted in millions of youth damaged so severely that failure in school, in home relationships, and in careers demands that mentors (parents, teachers, coaches, correctional personnel, pastors, and probation officers) provide the instruction (Laws of Eagles) that youth should receive from their biological fathers. Otherwise, U.S. teenagers likely will not be trained in basic skills needed for successful employment and marriage.

Compilation of the "Laws of Eagles" is the result of hundreds of hours spent with teens who were hungry for guidance from "a dad." The book is a tool chest from which youth can be taught essential life skills which fathers should teach.

These "Laws" are considered by the author to be the

essential concepts (philosophy of life) which youth desire and need to "soar like eagles."

The average attention span of teenagers is about six minutes before their minds begin to wander. Time-on-task increases in direct proportion to the perceived relevance of the material or content being read or taught. Each "Law of Eagles" is presented as a "relevant" item in the life of a teenager, and can be taught daily by biological or substitute dads in less than six minutes. Expanded time-on-task is dependent on the insight and skill of the teacher to elaborate on and apply the "Law" to personal circumstances relevant to the teenager's questions or circumstances.

The mentor should apply experiences, examples, and illustrations in one-on-one sessions and weekly group assemblies as applicable.

This book is designed for practical application by adults who are responsible for imparting to youth the essential virtues and principles necessary for success in the workplace, home, or community. *Teaching Eagles To Soar* is also appropriate as a gift for high school and college age youth.

As the author presented these laws in weekly school assemblies, each LAW was displayed on a screen via a transparency, projector, or power point program. Each student was given a print copy on which to make notes and retain in a three ring notebook. Each LAW was presented in a conversational "father-like" manner in which illustrations, vignettes, local incidents and examples were woven into the presentation as appropriate. Students were encouraged to ask questions, request examples and applications, and to request private appointments later to seek additional knowledge, understanding, or wisdom.

During one-on-one sessions the author asked a series of questions (see Appendix) designed to elicit information that would allow the author to "walk" the student through forgiveness (as applicable) of abusive people, restitution for vandalism or theft, seeking forgiveness for abusing others, anger, or "dealing with" rejection, ridicule, grief, bullying, depression, or incidents which contributed to or caused arrested learning.

The author discovered that teens made at-risk by adults' behavior (lifestyle) often demonstrated characteristics of rebellion and/or anger toward God, parents, teachers, or abusers. The combined application of probing questions based on *Teaching Eagles To Soar* enabled youth to "get on track" and to be set free to pursue adulthood confidently and successfully.

Laws are placed in alphabetical order to facilitate quick reference. Each appropriate LAW may be found easily as the student seeks guidance on specific issues such as anger, hopelessness, grief, courage, virtue, and thoughts. (Refer to table of contents for an alphabetical listing of Laws)

Recovery and training to soar begin only when external influences (responsible adults) effectively persuade youth to desire a lifestyle change little by little, thought by thought, act by act that replace toxic influences with positive choices.

Negative, toxic thoughts/acts, are neutralized or replaced by external, opposite positive influences brought into the life of youth via Laws of Eagles. A nurturing adult who demonstrates patient grace (eyes, posture, words) while applying *Teaching Eagles To Soar* can effectively help youth overcome the numerous consequences of being father-challenged. (See Figure 1)

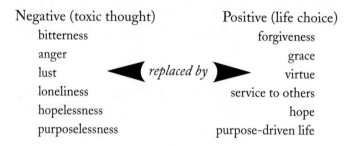

Negative (toxic thought)		Positive (life choice)
bitterness		forgiveness
anger		grace
lust	*replaced by*	virtue
loneliness		service to others
hopelessness		hope
purposelessness		purpose-driven life

Figure 1

The following stories about eagles illustrates
the purpose of this book.

A TALE OF TWO EAGLETS

THE FIRST EAGLET

The story is told of a farmer who found an eagle's egg and put it into the nest of a barnyard chicken. The eaglet hatched with the chicks and grew up with them. All his life, the eagle did what the chickens did. He scratched the dirt for seeds and insects to eat. He clucked and cackled. He flew no more than a few feet off the ground, in a chicken-like thrashing of wings and flurry of feathers.

One day the eagle saw a magnificent bird high in the cloudless sky. The eagle watched as the bird soared gracefully on the powerful wind currents, gliding through the air with scarcely a beat of its powerful wings. "What a beautiful bird," the young eagle said. "What is it?"

The chicken next to him said, "Why, that's an eagle—the king of all birds. But don't give him any mind. You could never be like him."

The young eagle returned to pecking the dirt for seeds, and he died thinking he was a barnyard chicken. What do you think of your own potential? It not only defines who you are today, but what you will be tomorrow. (Honor Books)

THE SECOND EAGLET

One day an adult eagle flew over a farm. On the ground was a flock of chickens pecking at corn scattered by the farmer. Among the chickens was a strange looking bird that pecked at the corn like the chickens, but the strange fowl obviously was not a chicken. The eagle circled lower for a better perspective. "What!" he exclaimed as he did a double take of the big bird among the chickens. "That is an eaglet! What is he doing with those chickens?" The grand eagle glided down to the farmyard and landed gracefully next to the eaglet who looked startled and started to run away with the frightened chickens. "Wait!" shouted the eagle.

"Why are you eating corn with these chickens?" The eaglet stopped to stare at the majestic eagle. Something about him sparked a feeling of dignity and pride in the eaglet. The older eagle asked again, "Why are you eating with chickens?"

The eaglet said in a matter-of-fact tone, "I am a chicken. Chickens eat corn." "Who said you are a chicken?" asked the eagle. "They did," gestured the eaglet toward the chickens huddled near the hen house.

"Look at me!" commanded the regal eagle. "Do I look like a chicken?" The eaglet gawked at the eagle and said, timidly, "No." The big eagle stretched his great wings and said, "Stretch your wings like mine."

The eaglet responded by unfolding his beautiful wings. "Now look at our wings. Do they look like chicken wings?" asked the eagle.

The eaglet's eyes enlarged as he looked first at his own wings then at those of the grand eagle. Again, he answered timidly, "No."

"Now look at my feet and your feet. Do they look like chicken feet?" "No," came the quiet reply. "Look at my head. Do I look like a chicken?" "No," responded the eaglet. "Look at yourself in that water pan," commanded the eagle, "Does that beak look like it belongs on a chicken?" "No, but they say I am a chicken," said the eaglet with a bewildered squawk.

"You are no chicken! You are an eagle, just like me. Now, when I spread my wings and fly toward the sky, you follow me. You belong up there in the clouds where eagles fly."

"Oh, but they said I could not fly," lamented the eaglet.

"Yes, you can!" snapped the eagle. "All eagles fly! Now, follow me!" he commanded as he lifted off the ground and soared to the top of the barn.

Just then the chickens erupted in a loud hysterical cry, "Leave him alone, he is a chicken! You have no right to tell him he can fly. He belongs here with us. You are just trying to embarrass him. What if he cannot do it? Let him alone!"

So, the eaglet plopped back down and stared forlornly at the great eagle as he glided back to the ground to stand beside the eaglet. The hysterical hens scattered back to the shadow of the barn and continued to scold the eaglet for listening to the admonitions of the great eagle.

The eagle turned his back to the hens and stared at the eaglet like a grand military commander. In a firm voice he said, "Son, you were created to soar, to fly among the mountain tops, to glide with the drifts, to build your nest on top of the world. You are an eagle. Can you not see what those hens have done to you? They have tried to make you into a lowly ground waddling, corn eating, barnyard chicken. They have lied to you, son! Can you not see that?"

The eaglet suddenly stood tall, stretched his wings, looked at the sky and said, "I always knew I was born to be more than they told me I could be."

Then, the chickens renewed their clamor, "No! No! Do not deceive yourself! You are a chicken! You cannot fly! You belong down here with us!"

The great eagle looked gently at the eaglet and said quietly, "Follow me to the mountain top, son. That is where you belong." He spread his great wings and soared. In the shadow of the great bird the eaglet flew up, up, up among the mountain tops where eagles were created to soar!

(Anonymous)

DEFINITION OF TERMS

Arrested Learning: the cessation or obstruction of learning and maturation from a specific moment in time when a traumatic event occurred such that the person's soul (mind, will, emotions) "froze" at the age of the incident [i.e. rape, auto accident, divorce of parents, death of parent/sibling, exposure to toxins (formaldehyde, mercury, lead.), physical assault, exposure to traumatizing fear or other mental input].

Bitterness: the willful, mental choice to hold a grudge, hatred, or anger toward another person who is perceived to be (or actually is) an abuser, adulterer, or accuser. Bitterness blocks freedom of thoughts as it constricts brain cells and nerve connections.

Fatherlessness: the condition in which a child does not have routine, daily guidance from his/her biological father.

Forgiveness: the act of forgiving a person for such things as abuse, theft, slander, gossip, rejection, assault, divorce, adultery—the acts which tempt a victim to be angry, bitter, or depressed. Forgiveness ("Please forgive me"), ("I forgive you") releases the soul.

Lifestyle: the choices a person makes about music, litera-ture, peers, finances, career, religion, activities, hobbies, residence, relationships, etc.

Mentor: a male role model who stands in place of a father to teach Laws of Eagles.

Toxic Influence: thoughts, ideas, suggestions, acts or images that weaken character and damage a person's potential for fulfillment.

Soar: to pursue a noble goal with a clear conscience, free of toxic restraints, adultery, rape, robbery, gossip, bullying, embezzlement, fraud, etc.

Victim mentality: the willful negative choice to remain a victim of a past incident rather than forgiving and "moving on" with life by assuming personal responsibility for finances, education, career, tasks, health, relationships, faith, etc.

THE LAW OF ADDICTION

Addiction is the result of grief.

Grief is the result of loss of loved ones and/or abuse by a stranger or trusted person.

Grief leads to depression as the person's thoughts focus on the abuse or loss of a relationship.

Focus on grief leads to anger, addiction, and bitterness.

Addiction tends to go away as the grieving person forgives the person(s) who abused or abandoned.

Forgiveness gives freedom from toxic thoughts, anger, grief, and bitterness—and leads to deliverance from addiction.

The most significant words in life for an addict are, "Please forgive me" and "I am sorry" for his/her own actions and "I forgive you" for the actions of abusers. Such words take away the excuse or reason to be addicted.

THE LAW OF ADMISSION, APOLOGY, & FORGIVENESS

Resolution of conflict and elimination of bitterness, rest upon admission, apology, and forgiveness for actions (by or against a person).

- Suppress pride. Say, "I'm sorry; please forgive me."
- Demonstrate humility/meekness. Say, "I forgive you for (specific action/abuse).

People who admit their faults and ask forgiveness in conflict or neglect of responsibility remove the argument against them and open a door to resolution or conciliation.

People who refuse to forgive others live with bitterness and anger, which restrict freedom and joy. Forgiving someone for an abuse is the first step to freedom from toxic thoughts that restrict success.

Forgiveness sets you free to soar!

Forgive others as you would have them forgive you. To forgive is to set both of you free to pursue noble dreams!

THE LAW OF
AFFIRMATION & APPROVAL

We become the type of people others affirm us to be.

We are affirmed by the people to whom we surrender our souls (mind, will, emotions).

We try to become like the people who affirm us and the people we admire.

We are shaped, formed and guided by affirmations of our dress, conduct, and companions. We tend to accept the attire, friends, activities, and physical attributes which our peers or heroes affirm.

People who constantly seek affirmations in order to feel secure struggle to find personal identity or life purpose. People with a sense of purpose appreciate, but do not rely upon, affirmations by others.

Everyone wants approval from peers, parents, spouse, employer, teachers.

Women respond better to approval and acceptance than criticism. Men need clear "orders" and job descriptions so that achievement is its own expression of approval.

(Dis)Approval is expressed in the forms of words, (spoken, sung, or written), eyes, posture, mouth (smile, pressed lips, frown).

Goals, tasks, and assignments should be achievable so that approval is highly probable.

Our own expressions of approval or disapproval of other people should be made with consideration of how we would feel or respond

Disapproval is positive and negative. Wrong choices should be subject to disapproval by those in authority over us. Disapproval of our wrong behavior is a positive thing for us.

Others affirm/influence us through: activities, attitude, morals, companions, attire, mentoring, and life goals/purpose. We become what we allow others to affirm who we are. We become a person of noble purpose by being with/like people who affirm our best qualities. Problems usually are the consequences of allowing negative people to affirm our lifestyle. (See Figure 2)

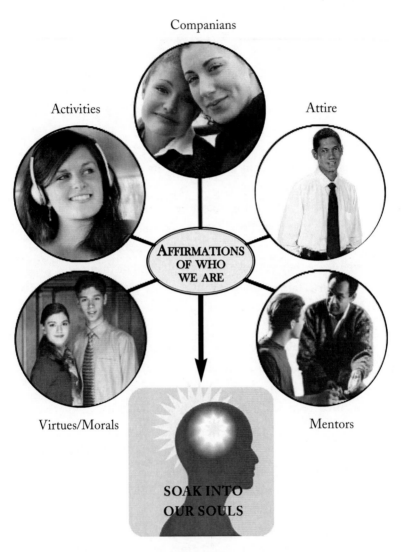

Companians

Activities

Attire

AFFIRMATIONS
OF WHO
WE ARE

Virtues/Morals

Mentors

SOAK INTO
OUR SOULS

Figure 2

THE LAW OF ANGER

Anger is expressed in words, thoughts, and actions, based on a victim mentality.

People express anger as a defense mechanism based on pride that does not like to be challenged or upstaged.

Young men and women will often flare in anger whenever they perceive to be challenged or insulted.

Most fights among youth result from words that ridicule, insult, or challenge a sense of self- image or self-worth.

People who live only for rights, praise, power, or popularity, are easily offended and angered.

People committed to a noble cause seldom feel justified to be angry at people who live with mediocre lifestyles.

A man whose thoughts are on lofty dreams seldom is angry with people of simple minds.

People whose minds entertain little ideals become angry easily at little things.

Avoid the company of angry people.

Don't pillow your head before you resolve any anger toward others. Forgive them and move on to the next step you need to take to soar like an eagle.

THE LAW OF AUTHORITY

Everyone is under authority.

People who honor authority experience success, protection, fulfillment, and freedom.

Authority umbrellas in life include God, parents, teachers, police, mentors, and employers. They protect us against abuse and harmful information and actions by others.

All umbrellas (persons in authority) have imperfections and weaknesses (holes in their umbrellas - character).

Your responses to authority either patch holes (forgive and obey) or punch holes (resist, criticize, disobey) in your authority umbrella (protection in life).

Your obedient actions/attitudes that patch holes (in their character weaknesses) include:

- Humility, forgiveness, virtues, obedience

Your actions/attitudes that punch holes in your protective umbrella include:

- Anger, involvement in pornography, extra-marital affairs, substance abuse, disobedience

Authority umbrellas over us (God, parents, teachers,

ministers, mentors, and employers) protect us by providing:

- Nutrition—making sure our bodies function well.

- Security—affirming a sense of safety.

- Instruction—teaching virtues/principles that make us good.

- Rest—making sure we get 8–10 hours of sleep daily.

- Guidance—helping us to see the truth and the right way.

- Training—assigning daily responsibilities: shoes and clothes in proper places—dressed for school/breakfast on time—meal with family (at least one daily)—homework completed/at school on time.

- Relief from stress—safe schools/homes are sanctuaries with "ears" to listen and loved ones to guide wisely.

- Healing from abuse and neglect—forgiving fathers for abandoning/asking forgiveness for anger/rebellion against authority (parents, teachers, employers).

- Fortification against predators—vulnerability signals are transmitted by our posture, eyes, mouth, attire, peers, language.

- Opportunities for involvement in noble causes give life purpose: a purpose-driven life engages our energy toward a goal and away from temptations to be careless.

- Exposure to model families/mentors: positive literature/media/activities—local faith-based entities/programs.

- Opportunity for the development of communication skills: answering softly to others turns away wrath—making an appeal to authority opens doors to promotion and success—listening with body, soul and spirit makes us wise and confident.

Laws and rules are for our protection.

A young person who rejects protection is exposed to danger.

People who do not follow orders can not lead others.

A sure sign of maturity is to live under authority.

(See Figure 3)

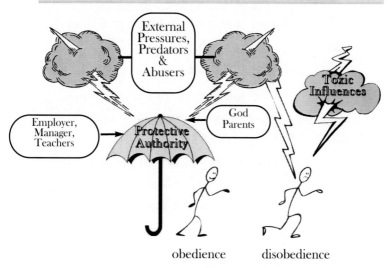

Figure 3

THE LAW OF BEGINNING

You become who you think you are. Begin today becoming who you were destined (want) to be.

1. Forget and forsake past abuses ... they only haunt you.

2. Appreciate present gifts of life ... they give joy and strength (school, health, caregivers, grace).

3. Be the person you wish others had been for you.

4. Set your desires on noble goals ... they will pull you past present negative conditions and relationships.

5. Work at being the person you were designed to be; stay away from people who try to degrade your virtues, values, and principles.

6. Resist and avoid people who would or could abuse or use you. Get away from them!

7. Seek wisdom and virtue ... they strengthen your ability to persevere.

8. Begin today thinking better than you thought yesterday - reject toxic thoughts or suggestions. Force yourself to reject negative thoughts; replace them with positive thoughts that lead you closer to your life purpose ... to soar like an eagle!

THE LAW OF BELIEF

BELIEF IS THE FOUNDATION OF *HOPE*.

1. What we believe about ourselves and our future drives our thoughts and responses. We are what we believe.

2. Belief is mere fantasy until we act responsibly to bring to pass a definite plan to fulfill our dreams.

3. Belief is fed from external factors through our five senses—what we see, hear, touch, taste, smell.

4. Belief is the sum total of what we allow to enter (or stay) in our mind, will, and emotions.

5. We become what/who we believe we are because we seek or receive into our souls the things (ideas, facts, lies, promises, etc.) which we willingly accept.

6. Some data should not be accepted into our belief system. (Turn away your eyes, refuse to taste, change the channel, walk away.)

7. Belief is a matter of the soul (mind, will, emotions), but also affects our body and spirit.

8. Belief is formed through knowledge (data), understanding (relationships among data) and wisdom (living by principles and virtues) which provide discernment and character.

THE LAW OF A BETTER LIFE

(GOOD, BETTER, BEST)

Life gets better when we get better. Nothing changes until we change something within ourselves.

Life is where you are; running away to another place only relocates your problems. You have to face them realistically regardless of how unfair or difficult they are. Life is often a matter of selecting the "best" of bad choices. That is when you need wisdom.

Problems are related to either: 1) Body—physical health or stature; 2) Soul—mind, will, emotions; 3) Spirit—God-consciousness; belief in the national motto, "In God We Trust," makes life best!

Life decisions/choices based on only one or two of these dimensions (body, soul, or spirit) are unstable.

Life gets better as (while) we build a new lifestyle around all three dimensions (body, soul, spirit): 1) Healthy intake of food and exercise; abstinence from drugs, alcohol, and promiscuity = a healthy body; 2) Feeding the soul with "good stuff" and avoiding "bad stuff" (sensual, demonic, violent) = a healthy mind/thoughts; 3) Feeding the spirit with wisdom, knowledge, and understanding = a healthy spirit (clear conscience that generates wise choices).

The *Secret To Success* is courage to avoid people, acts, places, and thoughts that reflect life we don't want to repeat. You become a "new person" as you practice a new (different) lifestyle based on goodness. You are at your best when living for the benefit of others. Your life tomorrow will be better than your life today when you act with your best character.

THE LAW OF
BIRTH, LIFE & DEATH

Life begins at conception.

Human life consists of three areas:

- Body: (bone, tissue, blood)

- Soul: (mind, will, emotions)

- Spirit: (God, eternity)

A happy, successful, and healthy person understands and exercises all three areas of human life.

Who we are in life is determined by our thoughts, beliefs, and choices about the past, present, and future. Our physical conception and birth were determined for us by parents. We have no choice about our skin, eyes, hair, nose, bone structure, personality, or talents. Our present choices affect life and death. Past choices affect present and future consequences on body, soul, and spirit. Man's greatest life challenge is to forgive the past, virtuously live in the present, and diligently prepare for the future.

(See Figure 4)

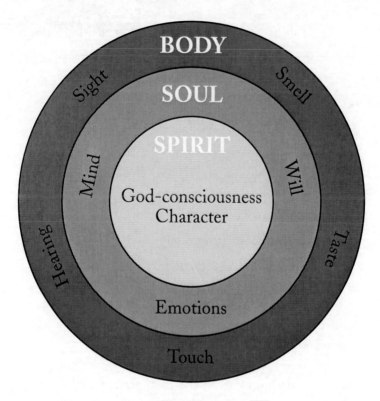

Figure 4

We begin life with circumstances over which we have no control. We do, however, have choices along the road of life. (See Figure 5)

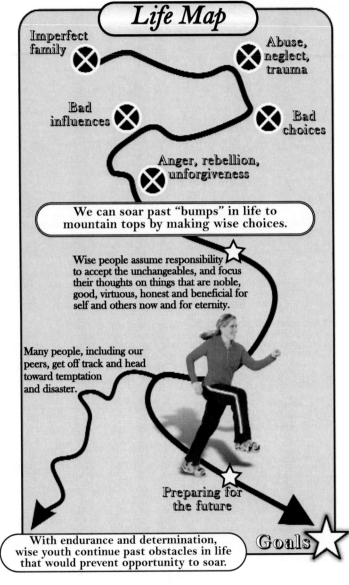

Figure 5

THE LAW OF BONDING

Bonding is an essential human need.

Bonding is the uniting of two souls in virtue and hope.

Hope is born and sustained with bonding between youth and their parents, care givers, teachers, and mentors (umbrellas of protection).

People who experience rejection (absence of bonding in womb/childhood) tend to be depressed, angry, purposeless, and restless.

People who experience bonding tend to demonstrate a sense of confidence, meaning, self-acceptance, and life purpose.

Children who are hugged daily by virtuous mentors usually have a head start on success.

The best formula for shaping a life is to bond it to virtue, hope, affirmation, love, gratitude, and noble life purpose.

THE LAW OF BOUNDARIES

Boundaries are fences that define our limits while directing our focus on goals.

Civil laws are fences that force us to stay within social boundaries.

Without boundaries, man naturally wanders off course, often to destruction or harm to self and others.

Self-restraint based on moral character, virtue, honesty, integrity, and noble purposes is the most effective boundary for mankind.

Men of lust, hate, anger, bitterness, selfishness, and vengeance, require boundaries of restraint enforced by society (prison).

A clear conscience toward God and people is the secret to living with freedom from civil boundaries.

Men of integrity are "free" because they require few man-imposed (man-made) boundaries.

The Ten Commandments are the basic boundaries for mankind; men who obey them live in physical, emotional, and spiritual freedom.

THE TEN COMMANDMENTS ARE THE MOST EFFECTIVE BOUNDARIES FOR SOCIETY:

"And God spoke all these words, saying: 'I am the LORD your God...

1: 'You shall have no other gods before Me.'

2: 'You shall not make for yourself a carved image—any likeness of anything that is in heaven above, or that is in the earth beneath, or that is in the water under the earth.'

3: 'You shall not take the name of the Lord your God in vain.'

4: 'Remember the Sabbath day, to keep it holy.'

5: 'Honor your father and your mother.'

6: 'You shall not murder.'

7: 'You shall not commit adultery.'

8: 'You shall not steal.'

9: 'You shall not bear false witness against your neighbor.'

10: 'You shall not covet your neighbor's house; you shall not covet your neighbor's wife, nor his male servant, nor his female servant, nor his ox, nor his donkey, nor anything that is your neighbor's.'

Jesus was once asked about the most effective law: "Teacher, which is the greatest commandment in the Law?" Jesus replied, "Love the Lord your God with all your heart and with all your soul and with all your mind. This is the first and greatest commandment. And the second is like it: Love your neighbor as yourself. All the Law and the Prophets hang on these two commandments."

Jesus was telling his followers that boundaries start in the heart. If a person loves God and loves people, then he/she has the ability to control him/herself and will need few external controls.

THE LAW OF A BROKEN HEART

The heart is where thoughts are processed from the mind, will, and emotions to the rest of the body.

Thoughts, habits, and acts begin in the soul (mind, will, emotions) and are filtered through the heart.

People say, "I have a broken heart," because of loss of a friend, family member, pet, or dream.

Consequently, the person feels sad, low on energy, hopeless, even depressed; the body's electrical-chemical system shuts down (because the heart is impacted with toxic thoughts and electrical-chemical imbalances).

Time itself can help heal a "broken heart." Because the body wants to survive so strongly, the mind begins to seek escape routes through external stimulation (new interests, forgiveness, helping others) on awareness that, "when one door closes, God opens another."

- Common toxic thoughts relating to a broken heart must be replaced:

Old Toxic Thought	New Virtuous Thought
* you are no good	* you are designed for good things
* it's all your fault	* fault is usually shared
* you are stupid	* you are equipped to make wise choices
* life stinks	* life is full of opportunities
* no one likes me	* people whose needs you meet appreciate you
* no one can be happy	* joy is my choice
* no one else cares for me	* the world is full of people with whom I can share my heart

- Thoughts enter the brain, pass through the heart, and affect its health and the person's strength to make wise choices.

- Toxic thoughts really do cause a person to experience a "broken heart."

- A broken heart can lead a person to make unwise decisions because the body fails to function properly (electronically and chemically) in a "broken" condition.

- The solution to a broken heart is to renew it—to get a "new heart" (not physically, but spiritually and emotionally) by replacing toxic thoughts with virtuous thoughts.

- The old lifestyle of toxic thoughts and habits will pass away when new thoughts based on virtue, forgiveness, hope, and noble goals build new emotional pathways through the heart. The new nerve pathways actually renew the heart.

- God is in the business of mending broken hearts.

THE LAW OF CAUSE AND EFFECT

Every act produces a similar effect or consequence.

- We reap what we sow.

- Do unto others as you would have them do unto you.

- Kindness begets kindness.

- Forgiveness encourages forgiveness.

- Anger produces angry responses.

- Vengeance leads to retaliation.

- Abusive acts earn abuse.

- Honesty generates honesty in return.

The greater force (cause) determines the effect (direction).

- Intake affects output.

- Pain affects judgment.

People who have a false sense of immunity from consequences act irresponsibly (cause), only to experience negative consequences (effects) from reckless life choices. Life has a way of arriving at balance only when we deliberately balance bad choices with better ones. (See Figure 6)

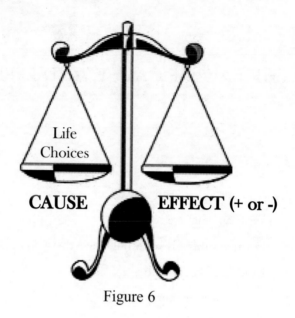

Figure 6

THE LAW OF CHAMPIONS

CHAMPIONS ARE:

- *Consistent* in daily responsibilities (David continued to feed his father's sheep, practice and play the harp, and carry his brothers' lunches, all after being anointed king).

- *Challengers* of evil and those who oppose what is right (not intimidated by the "impossible"). (Ronald Reagan opposed the "evil empire" of communism until the Berlin wall was torn down.)

- *Committed* in spite of ridicule from authority, family, strangers. (David was a "mere" shepherd, harp player, lunch boy and endured ridicule from his older brothers and King Saul.)

- *Courageous* in the face of danger because God is his source of confidence. (George Washington and Winston Churchill exercised faith in God to oppose tyranny.) Compassionate in meeting the needs of others (Mother Teresa helped orphans, widows and the destitute)

- *Covenant* holders - they are faithful in marriage, duty, and employment.

THE LAW OF CHARACTER

Character determines destiny.

Integrity is the basis of moral character.

Integrity is the soul's commitment to do what is best for a noble cause in spite of physical circumstances.

People of character live free of worry about consequences for bad choices.

Character says "NO" to negative acts (character keeps the soul free of clutter).

Character is enhanced or damaged by choices.

Daily we establish life priorities based on our character and the character of associates, peers, role models, mentors, and others in authority over us.

People of good character sleep with clear conscience.

Life is much easier when directed by virtuous character.

THE LAW OF CHEATING

To cheat means to use dishonesty to obtain an advantage on an exam, on a daily assignment, or in a monetary exchange. It may also mean unfaithfulness to a spouse. In any situation, the cheater loses because … cheaters never win, and winners never cheat.

Good or noble character forbids you to cheat on assignments, exams, taxes, a spouse, or tithes.

Cheaters are untrustworthy.

A noble man would rather lose property or money rather than his reputation.

To cheat is to sacrifice integrity in exchange for temporary pleasure or monetary gain.

Each act of cheating reduces a man's temperament to live trustworthily.

People who cheat on the "little things" usually cheat on the "big things" as well.

Purpose never to cheat!

THE LAW OF CHRISTMAS

Christmas is among the world's most popular holidays. Christmas is the formal recognition of the advent of Jesus, whose birth is the accepted time upon which all calendars are based (B.C. and A.D.).

Christmas is traditionally a time of rejoicing, celebration, family gatherings, and expressions of love through cards and gifts. Christmas is also a time of sorrow for some people who live in circumstances that challenge expressions of joy: poverty, hopelessness, strife, brokenness, debt, loss of family, failure, prison, death of a dream, etc.

Christmas is also a time when people reflect on basic questions, such as:

1. *Where did I come from?*

2. *Why am I here?*

3. *Where is my life going?*

4. *What do I need to change?*

5. *Who do I let influence me?*

Christmas is what we make it, depending on our perspective on life. We have joy if we have a spirit of gratitude for life, regardless of circumstances.

We have sorrow if we have a victim mentality and focus on "me, myself and I." As you think of others, remember that Christmas is not a time to go in financial debt. (The joy of giving fades under the weight of debts.) Joy is found in giving out of your limited or abundant resources.

Be creative as you think about the people to whom you would like to give gifts. If your resources are limited, you can give time to others (reading, helping, listening, mowing, cleaning, organizing, etc). You can make simple gifts: cards, book ends, paper weights, letter openers, scrap books, photo albums, wall plaques, wild flower arrangements, ear rings, etc. You can spend wisely according to your savings.

Our worth is not determined by the value or quantity of gifts we receive or give. It is determined by our sense of life purpose. Our worth increases as we give to others out of our resources.

THE LAW OF THE CIRCLE

What goes around comes around. Life is like a circle; it can be continuous or broken by choices.

The family circle is a term used to define unity among a husband, wife, and children.

Trauma occurs when the family circle is broken by death or divorce.

A broken circle breaks the unity of relationships, hope, confidence, and thinking process.

Life choices that demand immediate gratification (sex, tobacco, drugs, alcohol) usually break the circle—resulting in negative consequences and brokenness ... and more grief!

People who demand happiness or sensual pleasure "now" make impulsive choices that break the circle: pre-marital/extra-marital relationships, drugs, theft, fighting, or pornography.

Broken circles are hard to repair. Repair results by "going back" to the root issue—to the moment the circle was broken by trauma or bad choices and hating the act so passionately that you never want to repeat it (in your circle) and forgiving the abuser (person with whom your circle was broken).

Forgiveness of abusers (circle breakers) and forsaking that lifestyle begins the healing process for you and the other person.

Every person determines the type of circle in which to live.

Complete circles are made of such lifestyle virtues/principles as integrity, faithfulness, unselfishness, commitment, purity, honesty, forgiveness, and goodness.

Wise people create relationships that make good circles and avoid lifestyles that break family circles.

Our "circle" of friends determines where we "roll along" in life; we tend to follow where they go, and they tend to tag along where we lead. They soar when we soar; they plummet when we fall.

THE LAW OF
A CLEAR CONSCIENCE

A clear conscience is the secret of freedom.

A cluttered conscience blocks focus on life purpose and relationships. Forgiveness of others clears our conscience and releases our minds to be creative, to learn, to pursue goals—to soar!

A cluttered (guilty) conscience is like shackles on the soul (mind, will, emotions). Guilt binds us to our past actions, limitations and impulses.

A life of virtue is the best road to a clear conscience.

A clear conscience keeps away nightmares, guilt, worry, and regret.

Help others keep a clear conscience—treat them with dignity and virtue.

Purpose never to do anything that would cause another person to be shackled by a cluttered conscience.

THE LAW OF
A CLUTTERED CONSCIENCE

Violations of the conscience distract our ability to concentrate on recovery processes and tasks, or to pursue noble goals.

Virtue is the strongest form of filter or prevention against soul clutter (guilty conscience).

Clearing the conscience of clutter rests on admission of fault and asking forgiveness.

[Note: faith-based groups seem to work effectively as sources for conscience-clearing.]

Purpose never to commit an act that would clutter the conscience of yourself or another person.

A true friend is one who helps other "Eagles" stay pure, clean and uncluttered.

THE LAW OF
COGNITIVE STAGES

People mature through the three cognitive stages of knowledge, understanding and wisdom.

Acquired knowledge is foundational to understanding life, and wisdom is the product of virtue, character, and understanding.

What we learn in school is known as knowledge. How we apply it to solve problems is called understanding. How we deal with life by application of Judeo-Christian principles is called wisdom. Most people mature toward wisdom in direct proportion to the amount of time they spend learning principles, virtues and values associated with the character of God.

Youth exposed to virtues and principles in their studies (knowledge) incline toward wisdom.

Success is attainable as people elevate their thoughts and values from knowledge (people-focus) to wisdom (God focus).

Wisdom directs noble life purpose and expands life options.

Your focus on these three dimensions of life (wisdom, understanding and knowledge) determine the kind of person you are, and the altitude to which you soar!

(See Figure 7)

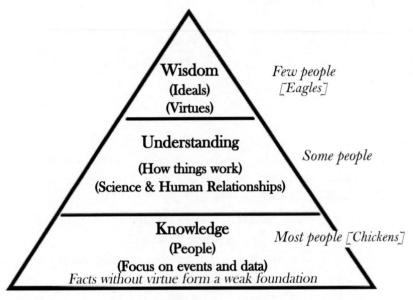

Figure 7

THE LAW OF
COMMUNICATION

We communicate beliefs, confidence, goals, wisdom, emotions and guilt, through our eyes, words, attire, posture, and peers with whom we associate.

We communicate by the way we carry ourselves ... our posture while standing, sitting or walking.

A smile on lips and eyes that twinkle convey a pleasant life with purpose.

A wrinkled brow conveys anger, doubt, stress, grief, bitterness, or worry.

A good, upright posture conveys confidence. By sitting upright, we are more alert and focused.

Words of praise and appreciation engage people around you.

A stooped, hang-shouldered posture conveys lack of confidence and vulnerability to predators.

A firm handshake and steady eye contact communicate confidence.

To be sharp, you have to dress sharp.

A sharp dresser communicates confidence and life purpose. Sloppy dress (attire) communicates laziness, neglect of what is appropriate, and a lack of motivation or purpose.

How we walk communicates our sense of life purpose and confidence.

What we think determines what we communicate.

A good vocabulary increases our communication skills and confidence, and opens doors of opportunity.

Remember, your friends communicate to others who you think you are.

THE LAW OF COMPENSATION

Wise people learn to compensate for lack of natural talent to accomplish noble goals.

Wise people who experience sorrow, pain or solitude turn their energy and interests to other challenges and thus accomplish achievements which otherwise may never have been attempted while in comfort, satisfaction, or pleasure.

Such people compensate for their emptiness, pain, or needs by focusing on tasks that demand attention.

Their loss, need, or malady becomes the catalyst that compels action in another direction or endeavor.

Abraham Lincoln was such a man—turning political defeat, loss of parents, financial disaster and physical unattractiveness into driving forces that guided America through the awful effects of the Civil War and effectuated freedom for slaves.

Gladys Aylward was an example of a person who compensated for rejection by the world, to become world famous for her heroic rescue of Chinese orphans.

Winston Churchill was rejected by his parents, yet he compensated for his solitude by turning his attention to learning to command the English language. As

Prime Minister of England during World War II, Mr. Churchill's command of words inspired, encouraged and fortified England to reject Germany.

Wise people do not accept challenges as excuses to be victims; they compensate!

THE LAW OF DAILY DECISIONS

Successful people make a few critical decisions early in life:

- To be grateful for what they have

- To think positively and optimistically

- To abstain from abusing body, soul, or spirit of themselves and others

- To begin and end each day reading material that strengthens their character

- To improve skills that make them more marketable

- To respect and honor other people in such a way that personal contact improves their options in life

- To honor family, country, and God

- To complete responsibilities and duties

- To plan today for tomorrow (daily write down at least five tasks and/or responsibilities which need to be completed tomorrow).

THE LAW OF
DAILY PLANNED PERSISTENCE

Recovery from pain or achievement of goals begins today by finishing at least one definite increment toward a goal or dream.

From here to anywhere is by planned, persistent steps. Persistence can be as simple as:

1. To say "NO" to a negative thought, suggestion or invitation.

2. To finish a specific responsibility—NOW!

3. To walk away from provocation immediately!

4. To express gratitude—NOW!

Don't put off today responsibilities you are tempted to delay.

Successful people plan their lives and live their plans.

Each morning:

1. Make your bed and put away shoes and clothes;

2. Dress and be at breakfast ahead of anyone else;

3. Arrive at school or work at least five minutes early;

4. Take breaks on time (not earlier or later than expected);

5. Stay focused on your responsibilities until time to clock out;

6. Take time to write down your top five priorities for tomorrow.

Each night:

1. Greet family members courteously and attentively;

2. Arrive at the dinner table clean and on time:

3. Read a portion of a good book that strengthens your character;

4. Go to sleep early so you get at least eight hours of rest.

A man who completes at least one daily goal toward his dream will eventually reach it; those men who complete more than one daily goal reach their dreams faster.

To try and fail a task is not shameful; not to plan or try is dreadful!

A rancher plants one fence post at a time; eventually, he forms a pasture in which to place his livestock (and thereby earn his living).

THE LAW OF
DATING AND COURTING

Youth naturally want companionship with the opposite gender.

Hormones dictate interest in getting to know a person to whom you are attracted.

Dating is not the same as "courting" with intent to marry.

Traditionally, couples who share common interests arrange with their parents to meet under chaperoned conditions to engage in conversation or social activities based on common interests in careers, hobbies, and responsibilities. This is called courting.

A "date" is too often interpreted as an opportunity to explore sexual curiosity or pleasure ("Let's date, but not wait" is a certain formula for cluttered conscience, emotional pain and probable pregnancy and/or disease).

Youth who date for sexual reasons seldom experience fulfilling marriages, but often do experience disease, unplanned pregnancy, and unfulfilled dreams...and a truck load of grief!

Wise youth do not base their sense of worth on dating and sexual partners. Insecure youth seek companionship often at the expense of purity and reputation.

Couples who date alone usually eventually engage in premarital sex: boys pressure girls with promises of "I love you" and girls seek emotional fulfillment through sensuality (attire, actions).

The average man says "I love you" to seven girls whom he pressures for sex before marriage or "living together."

The average girl "gives" her heart and body to at least two boys before she marries—and always regrets having done so.

THE LAW OF DEATH

Life is a vapor and uncertain, except this: all men and women die (some in youth, some in old age, but all die).

With life is the reality of eventual, sometimes sudden, death.

Death is appointed unto all men, then accountability and judgment for how they lived on Earth.

Wise people consider the brevity of life and live daily in such a lifestyle that death is not a fearful event.

Sorrow is felt by the survivors not only over loss, but over the nagging thought that the deceased person may not have made sure of eternal consequences or an eternal reunion with loved ones.

Every known culture has a heritage of life and death—and a legacy of eternity (life after death/after-death destination).

Wise people consider life and seek answers on how to face death.

The Bible is the most accepted source on life, death, and eternity.

(See Figure 8)

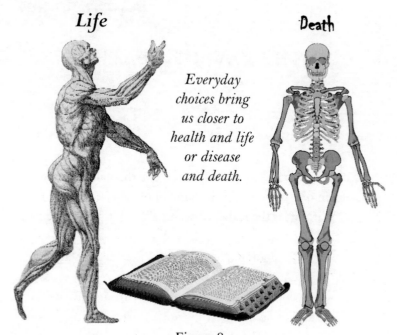

Life

Death

Everyday choices bring us closer to health and life or disease and death.

Figure 8

THE LAW OF DEPENDENCY

Man was created with dependency on love. Love is different than lust. Love gives to the needs of others without expecting anything in payment/return. Lust takes from others (their purity, confidence, integrity) in an attempt to fill the need for love.

People who experience trauma associated with the absence of love, attempt to become independent through false substitutes for reality; they often abuse:

- physical relationships

- drugs, alcohol, tobacco

- pornography

- homosexual acts

People who "make love" outside of marriage often end up with consequences that make persons dependent on others for food, shelter and clothing.

Love casts out fear of rejection. Love is hard to reject. We depend on people who love us. People who love us should be able to depend on us to act in their best interest.

Wise people depend on integrity and virtue to provide stability and true love.

The highest compliment is "I know I can depend on you to fulfill responsibilities with integrity!"

THE LAW OF DEPRESSION

People become depressed when they sense that their body, soul, or spirit has been abused.

Depression is the robber of happiness.

Depression is the result of a sense of loss (of dignity, purity, virtue) and a sense of hopelessness and grief.

Depression is emotional conflict (mind, will, emotions) in the soul and cannot be cured through physical stimulants (drugs, sex, or irresponsible or impulsive actions).

Depression often is associated with abuse. Victims and/or perpetrators of abusive acts experience depression from a sense of grief, guilt, or remorse.

Depression is not "forever." It can be conquered through forgiveness of the abuser(s) and self, and rejection of toxic thoughts and "open doors" to a cluttered conscience, such as drugs, pornography, or fornication.

Depression is "emotional matter" that can be replaced with hope and optimism (positive thoughts). Virtue, wholesome thoughts, noble dreams and forgiveness drive away depression and addiction.

A person "made clean" through virtue (forgiveness, goodness, righteousness) is "released" from the grip of depression.

Forgiveness is the ultimate anti-depressant.

Focus on noble causes, that benefit others leaves no room for depression.

Gratitude with forgiveness drives out depression.

THE LAW OF DESIGN

You are designed for a purpose—created as an individual.

You are not an accident! You have purpose and destiny!

You have special DNA, talents and gifts that set you apart as unique.

Your design and purpose, when tied to virtue and character, equips you for success.

Success is application of your design to help others be all they can be…you were not designed to please or abuse yourself or other people.

People who you try to help or who try to help you will either bring out or limit your ability to succeed.

Your design is bent, shaped, or sharpened by the people, acts, words, and experiences in your life. Others either make or break your quest for success.

Don't try to be somebody else; to do so would be to infringe upon their design and confuse your own identity.

Basic questions people need to ask and answer are:

"Who am I?" [A unique person of worth.]

"Why am I here?" [To establish an eternal purpose.]

"What am I designed to accomplish on earth?" [A noble dream]

"How are my choices/friends affecting my design?"

"What changes do I need to make to fulfill my design?"

"With whom and how can I strengthen my design?"

THE LAW OF DESTINY

You have worth (attributes) to fulfill your destiny.

A sense of destiny focuses our daily thoughts and priorities.

People who have a sense of destiny live with daily purposes and priorities. They are dream seekers!

You were created with gifts, talents, and temperament designed to fulfill a destiny.

You are not an accident! Your DNA was designed to fulfill a positive life purpose.

People are happy and fulfilled only when living with a noble sense of purpose and destiny.

Daily choices are made in the shadow of your sense of purpose.

Every daily choice (act) takes you toward or away from your destiny. Daily decisions determine destiny.

Moral courage is the basis of reaching a noble destiny.

A sense of destiny involves:

- Purpose/dream/goal

- Faith to act when opportunities appear

- Action to complete responsibilities

- Courage to dare to do right when circumstances say "No"

- Vision of achievement

- Virtues to guide choices

- Persistence to complete a goal.

   (See Figure 9)

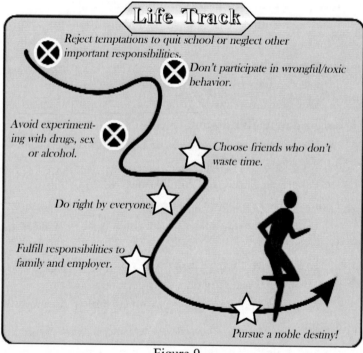

Figure 9

THE LAW OF DISTINCTION

You are wonderfully and marvelously made (DNA: designed for purpose and fulfillment)

You are exactly you—a unique person of worth and value.

Your distinctive qualities are displayed at their best when your life reflects virtue and purpose.

Avoid negative music, art, attire, and associates that would dull your distinction.

Literature and media attempt to shape you into a common image—like everyone else.

Don't try to "discover yourself" by associating with people who dislike who they are: (they slouch, dress sloppy, gripe, slur their speech, scoff at learning, claim to be victims of other people). Why would you want or allow such people to shape your life?

Pattern your life after people who are fulfilled achievers (people who give of themselves to benefit other people): they walk, talk, and stand with distinction.

People who dress like the crowd lose their distinctiveness.

The best way to distinguish yourself is to live in such a noble way that you are noticed.

THE LAW OF DOCUMENTS

Documents are written proof of your existence and activities. Important documents should be copied and kept in safe places (a metal box, a lockable briefcase, etc.).

Government documents include:

- Birth Certificate
- Military Records
- Social Security Card
- Tax Reports (Income, Sales)
- Driver's License/Identification card
- Titles for Vehicles and Property
- Marriage License
- Passport
- Adoption, guardianship, divorce

Institution documents include:

- Employment Identification (ID) cards/badges
- Baptismal Certificate

- Diploma, Certificate or Degree
- Insurance Policies
- Transcript of academic courses
- Will or Testament
- Loan Records
- Bank Records
- Stocks and Bonds
- News Articles
- Warranties/guarantees (vehicles, appliances, furniture)
- Health and medical records (blood type, diseases, injuries)
- Immunization records

THE LAW OF DREAMS

Dreams ought to be noble goals driven by passion to be fulfilled daily.

Dreams frame our daily priorities and choices.

Dreams pull us past less noble encounters that would distract us from fulfillment of our destiny.

A critical question must be asked by anyone who would be successful: "If I could not fail, what is my dream?"

A dreamer marches to a different drum beat; he hears the music of his dream and lets it guide his footsteps past distracters.

Dreamers are achievers because they believe in fulfilling a sense of purpose—they chose to live for something they are compelled to attain or capture.

People without a dream remain victims to temptations and complacency.

A dreamer covers his eyes and ears from temptation so he can focus on the music of his dreams.

Dare to dream!

Dare to soar to attain it!

THE LAW OF EAGLES

Eagles soar with other eagles; they don't:

- peck with chickens

- squabble with turkeys

- drift with buzzards

Eagles are majestic because they soar above common creatures.

Recovery of dreams occurs when common associations are replaced with noble companions (role models in songs, books, media, real life) who inspire us to greatness.

Eagles are not victims; they soar above circumstances. They dare to be nobler than others!

Eagles watch, wait, and soar in the shadow of lofty mountains, never staying long in valleys, depressions, or swamps.

Eagles are noble - and soar like it!

THE LAW OF EMANCIPATION FROM CHILDHOOD

Becoming an adult requires the putting away of dependence upon parents for providing essentials and making choices.

Attaining adulthood is both a legal process and a maturation process:

- At age 17, youth are considered adults for criminal actions.

- At age 18, youth are considered adults for military duty, personal accountability, voting, and financial debts.

- At age 21, youth are considered adults for holding public office and purchasing property and certain products.

Emancipation from adolescence is affected by:

- training, skills, initiative, personal character/maturity
- age (legal maturity)
- emergency events (loss of parents/trauma)

The more responsibility youth exercise with relationships and life choices (anticipating consequences), the more rapidly emancipation from childhood occurs.

Demand for personal, immediate gratification of physical desires prolongs emancipation and "adulthood" maturity. Immaturity enhances irresponsibility and leads to prolonged dependence on adults for basic needs.

(See Figure 10)

Mature emancipation is a process.

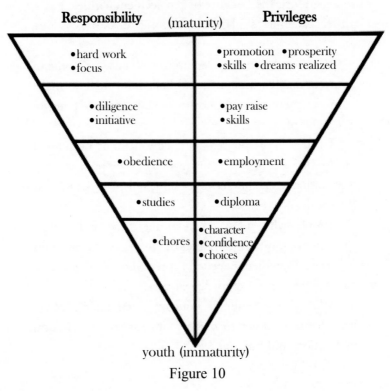

Responsibility   (maturity)   **Privileges**

- hard work
- focus

- promotion • prosperity
- skills • dreams realized

- diligence
- initiative

- pay raise
- skills

- obedience

- employment

- studies

- diploma

- chores

- character
- confidence
- choices

youth (immaturity)

Figure 10

THE LAW OF THE EMPTY CUP

Recovery from past abuses or experiences requires giving up some current lifestyle choices in order to create space to experience the benefits of replacement virtues, goals, attire, academics, skills, responsibilities, chastity, wisdom, etc.

We must be willing (required) to "pour out" some of our toxic habits, thoughts, and beliefs in order to make room for the mentor, authority, or counselor to "pour in" new content.

Until "old" is poured out, "new" cannot be poured in. We become new persons (eagles) as we pour out the habits, character, and desires of "chickens," "turkeys," and "buzzards."

People who insist on retaining their old habits, choices, grief, bitterness, anger or "rights" leave no room to receive ingredients needed for recovery from abuse or past failures, or to experience success.

Wise people willingly pour out their toxic lifestyle ingredients in order to make room for virtue, wisdom, instruction, and training.

(See Figure 11)

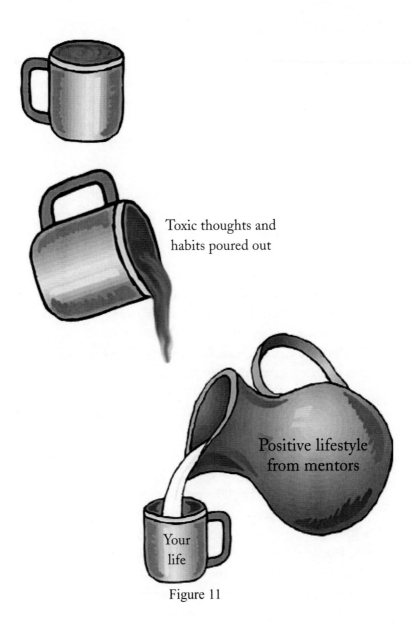

Toxic thoughts and
habits poured out

Positive lifestyle
from mentors

Your
life

Figure 11

THE LAW OF EXCEPTION

Most people believe they are the exception to life's rules.

Bad choices are made because people falsely presume that they are exempt from the negative consequences which affect other people. That is "unreality"; it is fantasy.

A major paradox in life is that people both want and reject God's omnipresence (the fact that He is everywhere), omnipotence (the fact that He is all powerful), and omniscience (the fact that He is all knowing).

Immature people want God to be awake when needed and to be asleep when disobeyed.

Wise people study to gain knowledge, understanding, and wisdom about the benefits and consequences of divine and civil laws.

Reality is that all mankind is under the same universal laws.

A sense of virtue enables people to make wise choices that keep them under the protective umbrella of laws/authority.

People who live in fantasy presumptuously exempt themselves from possible consequences of laws, but end up validating the consequences of disobedience to those laws.

A basic universal law is, "Be sure your disobedience will find you out."

THE LAW OF EXCUSES

Noble men don't make excuses for irresponsible decisions or careless acts.

People quick to make excuses are quick to avoid responsibility.

Excuses are feeble attempts to make a man appear successful.

Successful people don't make excuses for their circumstances or actions.

The best use of "excuse me" is when we accidently bump into a person. The worst use of "excuse me" is when we want to blame others for our faults.

People who constantly make excuses for failure to fulfill responsibilities develop a victim mentality that leads to perpetual dependence on other people to supply basic needs.

THE LAW OF EXTRA EFFORT

"When you give more than is demanded, you get more than you deserve."

Employees who start at minimum wage, stay there until they give maximum effort to their employer.

Noble work is honorable when done with excellent effort.

People who work only for a paycheck seldom are promoted.

Increased wages follow increased effort to increase profit for the employer. Effort is defined in initiative.

Employees who gain a good reputation for hard work also gain promotion and good wages.

Employers notice both diligence and negligence, and set wages accordingly.

A worker is worthy of his wages. He who does not work shall not earn wages.

THE LAW OF FALSE COMFORT

The natural response to emotional or physical pain is to find comfort.

Emotional pain causes a victim to desire relief from whatever source is nearby or available.

Abused people often seek immediate comfort from sources that leave the person with more pain (common-law relationships, one night stands, homosexuality, debt, drugs, etc.).

Because stress is part of physical or emotional pain, the body chemistry is disrupted, causing a desire for comfort.

That is why some people crave candy, sex, alcohol, or drugs to relieve emotional pain (discomfort).

Tragically, the "false" comfort often results in increased pain:

- candy—excess weight/fat/disease
- alcohol/drugs—addiction/dependency
- impulsive buying—debt/ruined financial credit
- sexual promiscuity—diseases, pregnancy, loss of purity, abuse

Often, further consequences of such actions result in:

- extra marital affairs—divorce, broken family, disease
- resignation/loss of job—unemployment/loss of career dream
- dropout from school—unemployable/unable to pursue life dream

Lasting comfort from pain occurs only when life choices and activities are altered as a result of new thoughts that build a new lifestyle.

Pain continues until the source is removed, replaced, or overpowered by a new source previously inaccessible in the old lifestyle of toxic peers, thoughts, habits, activities, and addictions (old ways poured out to make room for new habits).

Comfort comes when new thoughts (based on virtues, high aspirations, noble purpose) replace old thoughts to create new mental pathways that bring relief from emotional pain.

False substitutes never last. Real replacements open new paths in the brain to bring comfort.

Tragically, people who resort to daily "false comforts" (sex, food, drugs), seldom get relief from deep emotional pain.

People who seek or receive new thoughts, new virtues, new friends, and new lifestyles, usually find lasting comfort from pain.

THE LAW OF FATHERS

Fathers (biological and substitute) have responsibility toward youth to:

- *Affirm* motivational gifts and character.

- *Instruct* in knowledge, character, wisdom, skills, and financial management.

- *Prohibit* expressions of anger, rudeness, apathy, rebellion, defiance, selfishness, greed, sensuality, dishonesty, laziness and pride.

- *Discipline* for disobedience, cruelty, dishonesty, destruction, slothfulness, abuse, laziness, and neglect of duty.

- *Protect* from harm (physically, mentally, spiritually). *Provide* an example of a positive role model, adequate food, clothing and shelter, and opportunities to serve others.

"Make yourself into the person you wish your dad had been."
—Glenda Browder

EVERY CHILD LONGS FOR APPROVAL
AND LOVE FROM HIS/HER FATHER.

A man or boy should never engage in the "act of marriage" that could lead to fatherhood unless he is married to the woman with whom the "act" is shared.

A woman or girl should never engage in the "act of marriage" with a man who is not her lawful husband and legitimate father of the potential child.

A boy or man who would become a father by a girl who is not his lawful wife shames her and damages his own soul.

Fatherhood in marriage is wonderful; fatherhood in fornication or adultery is painful!

THE LAW OF FEAR

The presence of fear both preserves life and weakens life.

Survival of man and creatures rests in a natural reaction to fear of consequences.

Without fear of shame or punishment, humans commit foolish and hurtful acts against themselves or others.

The opposite of fear is trust. The secret to life is to fear some things (acts, people, substances) while trusting in virtue and the eternal source of power that can deliver us from that which we fear.

Our national motto is "In God We Trust." The founding fathers based that formula on a Bible verse which states, "The fear of the Lord is the beginning of wisdom"—wisdom is the ability to discern what is good and harmful, and then the ability to avoid fearful things, acts, or people.

It is wise to fear careless disregard of virtues, rules, or authority designed to protect us.

Men of virtue have little to fear from choices.

People live in fear when they live carelessly and irresponsibly.

Fear stifles creativity and thinking. Fear shuts down

our ability to be rational. Fear attacks our immune system, making us susceptible to viruses, allergies, panic attacks, and poor choices.

That which we fear comes to pass if we dwell on it (thoughts).

Fear steals creativity.

Fear is overcome by faith and courage (to act in the face of fear).

Fear misdirects our thoughts, emotions, perspectives, and feelings.

Fear affects judgment.

Fear damages our health (physical, mental, emotional, spiritual).

Formula for overcoming fear:

1. Acknowledge it

2. Face it down

3. Refuse to invest in the source (i.e. person, incident)

4. Conquer it (by replacing it with forgiveness/ optimism/gratitude/praise)

America's Founding Fathers conquered fear by trusting in Divine Providence. Our national motto, "In God We Trust" is the basis of America's courage to defend freedom to pursue happiness.

RESOURCES THAT ADDRESS FEAR

"Oh my God, I trust in you; let me not be ashamed, let not mine enemies triumph over me." (Psalm 25:2)

"O keep my soul and deliver me (from that which I fear); let me not be ashamed, for I put my trust in you." (Psalm 25:20)

"The Lord is my light and my salvation; what shall I fear? The Lord is the strength of my life; of whom shall I be afraid?" (Psalm 27:1)

"Perfect love never fails, is kind, patient, does not envy, is not proud, does not boast, does not behave rudely, is not selfish, is not easily provoked, does not think evil, is truthful, endures all things, is hopeful." (I Corinthians 15:4–8)

"There is no fear in love; but perfect love casteth out fear: because fear hath torment. He that feareth is not made perfect in love." (I John 4:18)

THE LAW OF FEELING
WELL OR ILL

Stress is the number one cause of illness - feeling badly (depression, physical health).

Stress is based on or related to:

1. Lack of forgiveness of/or bitterness toward another person

2. Grumbling, griping and fault-finding about circumstances

3. Anger toward a person or God

4. Association with negative peers/family

5. Negative or selfish desires and thoughts

6. Junk diet ("dead food")

7. Grief from loss of loved one or abuse from a trusted person

Source of healthy body, soul and spirit - feeling well:

1. Gratitude for little things in life

2. Laughter at wholesome experiences

3. Service to others

4. Clean and virtuous thoughts, acts and conversation

5. Nutritious food

6. National motto "In God We Trust"

7. Daily Exercise (20–30 minutes)

THE LAW OF
A FIRST IMPRESSION

You have only one opportunity to make a first impression.

How you dress tells others what you think of yourself and others.

The way you dress affects the way people think of you and the way you think about yourself.

A wise man dresses appropriately for the occasion.

A good impression is made by following a few simple practices: wear a belt that holds up your pants at the waist; wear a shirt with sleeves; tuck in your shirt; wear shoes that are clean and polished.

Wear a tie when appropriate (i.e. certain job interviews, special social events). (*See Law of the Necktie on how to tie a necktie)

Our motivation should be to give the impression that we are aware that how we dress is important.

THE LAW OF FLAWED DADS

Every father is flawed. Your dad and the fathers of your friends have flaws ... because they are human.

Every father was the son of a flawed father and tries to live up to or be different from their dads. You are flawed too ... as is every person!

Youth absorb parts of their dad's character: the good and the bad. The aspect they focus on or emulate sets their direction in life.

A youth who judges or dishonors his/her dad for his flaws tends to become like the dad in the process. Youth can't change their dads, but teens can purpose not to emulate the flaws of their dads. Youth are wise to place themselves under the umbrella of protection and counsel of men of integrity (if not their fathers, then other men of integrity).

Youth who chose to be victims of flawed dads usually become like their fathers.

Youth tend to react to their flawed fathers by disobedience and rebellion against authority (including mothers) in an effort to find meaning in life.

Flaws can be "patched" by prayer, instruction, forgiveness.

Youth who emulate good men and pursue noble purposes (rather than focusing on the absence of, or negative characteristics of flawed fathers) can overcome the flaws of their fathers.

A purpose-driven life of virtue experiences fulfillment, joy, and peace of mind and soul.

Live for something bigger than the toxic values, abuses, problems, peers, or disappointments of flawed men.

Overcoming the flaws of parents requires daily achievements (small steps of responsibility) leading toward a life driven by noble purposes.

The time to start living with purpose is today. Today is the first day of the rest of your life. What you focus on today is who you will be tomorrow… in spite of the flaws of your father.

Quit living "against" your dad or mom, and start living "for" something noble.

Become the kind of person you want your dad to be. (See Figure 12)

Figure 12

THE LAW OF FOCUS

People who focus on positive priorities succeed.

People who break their focus of energy on noble priorities become distracted from their goal or life purpose.

Distracters are the little things to which we give attention at the moment.

Distracters are usually encounters that offer momentary pleasure or relief from stress, loneliness, or pain.

A series of little distractions eventually force loss of focus on the things that really matter in life.

Wise people learn to walk away from distractions; they keep focused on their dream, goal, purpose. They learn to say "No" to toxic temptations (distractions).

THE LAW OF FRIENDS

Select friends wisely. Friends shape us and reflect who we are.

Friends should be persons who...

... *Motivate* us to achieve our best.

... *Protect* us from making wrong choices.

... *Inspire* us to noble goals.

... *Help* us be us (spiritually, physically, and mentally)

... *Expect* nothing from us but truth.

... *Take* time with us to smell the roses.

... *Bring* out our best qualities.

... *Direct* our financial resources toward our dream.

... *Focus* our interest on helping others.

Friends are those people with whom we share time, emotions, activities, resources.

Friends (peers) define who we are and what we believe, desire, and respect in life.

Real friends respect us enough to tell us the truth about the things we say or do.

Friends (peers) pressure us to conform to their standards of dress, beliefs, and values in order to confirm their own feelings of importance and security.

True friends bring out our best qualities while restraining expression of our negative qualities.

True friends can't be bought with money, favors, or privileges.

True friends do not expect anything in return for our friendship.

A good test of true friendship is to deny a request or demand for a favor, money, or privilege, then evaluate the "friendship" for sincerity or opportunism.

Be strong enough to walk away from a "friendship" ("peership") that requires you to act, speak or do anything that lowers your dignity, virtues, character, purity, integrity, or goals.

Some friends have opposite temperament, strengths and personalities that attract us. (We should be cautious not to let their dominant qualities determine who we are or what we believe, say, or do.)

Our values, appearance, beliefs, and personality attract the kind of persons we are or attempt to become.

Be the kind of friend your body, soul and spirit need in order for you to be your best.

Do not let your friends (peers) define you as anyone less than a person of integrity.

Select only "eagles" as your friends, and soar with them!

THE LAW OF FULFILLMENT

Every person was designed to fulfill a destiny.

Every person has dreams yet to be fulfilled.

A sense of incompleteness haunts everyone.

Tomorrow is always on the mind because everyone thinks about the future...what it holds, what will be experienced.

Fulfillment is the result of dreams pursued, purposes realized, and selfish desires denied.

Each task or goal accomplished simply becomes the base on which to build new dreams and goals to be fulfilled.

Life is empty for people who do not pursue dreams, goals or noble causes.

A vital aspect of fulfillment is periodic affirmations and encouragements from people we respect and admire.

Fulfillment is the result of persistence and self-discipline to accomplish little tasks which are stepping stones that open doors to a greater goal, cause, or dream.

A major component of fulfillment is the character to walk away from anyone who does not affirm your noble quest, and/or to reject any experience that could distract you from fulfilling your destiny, dream, goal or noble cause.

People who fulfill big dreams or accomplish great feats are guided by principles, virtues, and values above those practiced by average people.

Great achievements are accomplished by ordinary people who dream bigger and live higher than peers who simply live for pleasure, fun, or excitement. Dreamers soar like eagles!

THE LAW OF
GETTING RID OF ANGER

You cannot be "made" angry. Anger is a choice.

Some anger is justified. Anger to correct abuse against others is justified. Valiant soldiers acting in anger to defend freedom or oppose bullies are justified.

Venting anger because of something done or not done against you is not the proper focus of anger. Anger as an emotional release of bitterness is not justified.

Vengeful anger is usually expressed by cutting or harsh words or violent actions. "Getting back" through anger is unwise.

Avoid hanging out with angry people as a lifestyle.

Bitter anger eats away our lives.

Identify the source of your anger and deliberately put it away from you with forgiveness of the person who hurt or abused you.

Anger retained in your soul hurts you more than the person at whom your anger is addressed.

People tend to become like the person at whom anger is focused.

THE LAW OF GOD IN AMERICA

U.S. CULTURE HAS A HISTORY OF WORSHIP OF GOD.

The first document written in America was the *Mayflower Compact* which included the phrases, "In the name of God, Amen … by the grace of God … Having undertaken, for the glory of God, and advancement of the Christian faith…" The first book published in America was the *UpBiblum* compiled by Christian missionary, John Eliot, for the teaching of Native Americans, specifically the Algonquian tribes of the east coast. The book was a translation of important passages in the Bible, such as "The Lord's Prayer," the "Sermon on the Mount," and the "Ten Commandments."

The first American dictionary was compiled by Noah Webster and included biblical scripture references to accompany the definition of each word, such as the word, "property." The definition included references to God, such as, "The exclusive right of possessing, enjoying and disposing of a thing; ownership. In the beginning of the world, the Creator gave to man dominion over the earth, over the fish of the sea and the fowls of the air and over every living thing. This is the foundation of man's property in the earth and all its productions..."

The first songbook published in America was the *Bay Psalm Book* which was a collection of scripture verses put to music, such as Psalm 23.

The Declaration of Independence is sprinkled throughout with references to God, including the phrase, "We hold these truths to be self-evident, that all men are created equal, that they are endowed by their Creator with certain unalienable rights, that among these are Life, Liberty and the pursuit of Happiness..."

One of the first actions taken by the new U.S. Congress was to appropriate 20,000 Bibles for soldiers and their families.

America's first president, George Washington, took his oath of office while his hand rested on an open Bible, turned to the passage of Psalms 127:1. Washington's First Inaugural Address urged the American people never to forget God's hand in the creation of the United States. "...We ought to be no less persuaded that the propitious smiles of Heaven can never be expected on a nation that disregards the eternal rules of order and right which Heaven itself ordained...He has been pleased to favor the American people with opportunities...His divine blessing may be equally conspicuous in...the wise measures on which the success of this Government must depend."

The U.S. Pledge of Allegiance includes the phrase, "One nation under God." The presidential oath includes the phrase, "So help me God." The National Motto is,

"In God We Trust." The National Anthem includes the phrase, "In God is our Trust." Every state constitution includes references to God. U.S. coins and currency are stamped, "In God We Trust." Historic American holidays commemorate God's involvement in earth and the U.S. (Easter, Thanksgiving, and Christmas). The first amendment to the U.S. Constitution prohibits Congress from forbidding exercise of faith in God.

The U.S. Supreme Court issued a decree that students in public schools may:

- Say the Pledge of Allegiance aloud

- Display the National Motto (In God We Trust)

- Speak, illustrate (draw), write, or sing of God and faith in God

- Study or quote the Bible

- Pray alone or collectively; silently or aloud

- Share and express their faith in public or private gatherings, such as athletic events, graduation exercises, and yearbooks.

All of the above are permissible as long as:

- Such expressions of faith are not teacher-mandated and lead

- Such expressions of faith do not disrupt the educational process

- Such expressions are not vulgar, racist, or violent.

THE LAW OF GOOD

Happy people live for something good that will outlive death.

Men become good when they are influenced by good people or books.

Good character can't be stolen; it can only be given away.

You are a good person when you can laugh with joy through tears of sorrow when abused or neglected.

Don't just be good at what you do; be better, and when challenged or tempted to be bad, be your best!

Be captured by goodness; it will set you free!

Men who are good are strong; men are weak when they are bad.

People who focus on good thoughts avoid bad experiences and are free from bad habits.

THE LAW OF GOOD AND BAD

Wherever good is present, bad is, too.

Goodness is the universal force that urges men to achieve noble deeds opposed always by badness.

Good men build and protect communities. Bad men, motivated by greed, lust, power, or revenge, oppose goodness.

Goodness is best defined by the Golden Rule, "Do unto others as you would have others do unto you."

Wise people choose good friends and shun bad companions. Good friends tend to make us good. Bad companions corrupt our good intentions.

A universal law prevails, "Do good and you shall dwell safely and prosper."

A good man out of the treasures of his heart does good deeds.

A bad man out of the treasures of his heart does bad deeds.

Good friends tend to make us good. Bad companions corrupt our good intentions and distract us from noble dreams.

THE LAW OF GOOD HOMES

Strong homes are the result of purpose and application of God's laws.

One of His laws is *Forgiveness*: "And be kind one to another, tenderhearted, forgiving one another." (Ref. *Ephesians* 4:32)

Fifty percent of children in classrooms are from broken homes. Broken homes often include anger, bitterness, grief, lack of remorse for bad actions and a lack of forgiveness for the actions of others.

Fatherlessness (not living with a biological or adoptive father) is identified as a primary contributor to juvenile delinquent behavior and abuse of prescription drugs for ADHD, ADD, Bipolar, and depression.

Too many youth are turning out mediocre or delinquent because families do not desire good homes. Parents who demonstrate God-consciousness tend to parent effectively.

The first step to solving family conflicts is for the father (or head of the house) to set the national motto right in the middle of all family issues and build the family on it.

"In God We Trust" means we desire:

- Moral Absolutes
- Accountability for choices
- Noble Causes
- Orderly lifestyle
- Direction for living
- Privileges with Responsibility
- Love and respect for one another

. . . these are the characteristics of a good home.

THE LAW OF GOODNESS

Good people win!

A good conscience is the secret to good sleep.

Goodness and mercy follow people whose lifestyle is guided by wisdom, knowledge, and understanding.

Do good and you will dwell peacefully and with contentment.

Good people are respected and desired.

The public trusts and admires a good man or woman.

A good name (reputation) is better than wealth.

A good man is:

- trustworthy......... with money

- kind.................... toward others

- truthful.............. in speech

- loyal.................... to purpose (goals)

- obedient............. to authority

- gracious.............. toward strangers

- diligent............... in responsibilities

- wise.................... in choices

- dependable........ in conflict

A man with a good conscience is able to sleep peacefully and confidently.

THE LAW OF
GOOD HOUSEKEEPING

Good housekeeping involves more than spousal kindness, a broom, dishwasher, and vacuum cleaner. Most young married couples "mess up" their marriage in five basic areas beyond romance: records, keys, repairs, meals, and finances. The wise husband and wife team will agree to practice the following simple organizational procedures in their home.

KEYS—A key rack should be attached to the wall in a place where family members deposit keys immediately upon entering the home. The rack should include the following keys (with extra/spare keys) identified with tags: auto, house doors, storage shed, lawn mower, filing cabinet, tractor, desk, etc. as applicable. Plastic, colored rings can be purchased at a hardware store to color-code various keys for quick identification. This simple device prevents panic, frustration, and inconveniences.

RECORDS—A file box or two-drawer file cabinet should be set up to retain important original and photo copies of documents that will be needed at various times: marriage license, birth certificate, social security card, drivers license, baptismal certificate, diploma, college degree and transcript, award certificates, letters of recommendation, passport, property deeds, vehicle titles, will, inventory of property, investment accounts, charitable donations, insurance policies (health, auto, house, life, liability, etc), correspondence, resumes, warranties (refrigerator, air conditioner, computer, television, vacuum cleaner, toaster, oven, washing machine, dryer, etc.), photos, income tax forms, bank and credit card statements, receipts for utilities, car payments, house payments (rent or purchase), Note: in case of an emergency (fire, flood, tornado), this box should be "grabbed" and taken to a safe place.

BILLS TO PAY—A special place (drawer, file cabinet folder, shelf, stack tray) should be identified as the place where all invoices and bills are placed pending payment. The most common monthly bills are: utilities, cell phone, house phone, car payments, rent, insurance, credit cards, school loans, etc. The best procedure is to have two dividers or folders: one for the first half of the month and the other for the second half of the month. This allows you to pay bills before the expiration dates (and subsequent interest and late fees). You may want to keep the checkbook in the special place. Note: avoid credit card debts; always pay credit card balance in full before the invoice deadline!

TOOLS—Every house needs a small tool box with which to conduct repairs on appliances, lawn mower, toys, furniture, etc. The box should include at least the following items: hammer, tape measure, carpenter square, electric drill, pliers, wrench, screwdriver, socket set, plumber's tool, hacksaw, and carpenter saw. These tools allow you to conduct minor repairs, hang pictures, build crafts, repair leaky faucets, etc. A handy tool box is a great "tool" to save cash!

MEALS—Every household needs a comprehensive cookbook with recipes for nutritional foods for breakfast, lunch, dinner, and desserts. Family meals consisting of nutritious foods help keep a family healthy and cordial. Households in which both spouses work outside the home face temptations to "eat out" several days per week. The financial cost and damage to physical health from "fast foods" argue strongly for the couple to develop good meals rapidly. That's why a good cookbook is essential for good housekeeping!

THE LAW OF GRATITUDE

A spirit of gratitude inspires mental creativity to find solutions to current unfavorable circumstances.

People who focus on what they have rather than on what they do not have tend to experience peace of mind, contentment, fulfillment of life purpose, and attainment of goals.

People who willingly say "thank you" usually gain what they want in life.

People without a sense of gratitude tend to develop a victim/abuser mentality.

Gratitude is a noble attitude!

A person who does not express gratitude tends to be selfish, abusive, and demanding of others.

A grateful person is pleasant company.

(See Figure 13)

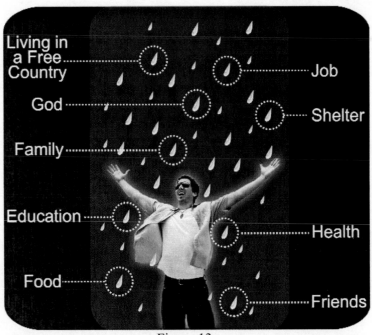

Figure 13

THE LAW OF HABITS

We are defined by our habits; they reflect who we are.

Habits determine our destiny (what we do today is foundational to who we are tomorrow).

Habits are the result of repeated, self-directed choices or repeated, external-directed training/conditioning.

Habits are acts done repetitiously over time.

Habits are the result of routine acts.

Habits are acts/behaviors done unconsciously.

Some habits form out of fear of reprisal from authority or rejection from a person with whom we have bonded.

Some habits/routines become safety buffers against accidents or abuse (lock doors/windows, turn off appliances, decline offers from strangers, etc.).

Habits can be formed or changed in 21 days.

Habits are addictive (shaping our words, acts, passions, desires—our life).

Habits develop easily, but are difficult to change.

Bad habits are hard on us (financially, spiritually, emotionally, physically).

Good habits make life easier by forming a protective shield around our inclinations, temptations, and affections.

Good habits cause us to make good choices automatically.

As you walk through life, habits of gratitude, honesty, integrity, fairness, gentleness, kindness, forgiveness, hard work, consideration of others, faith and hope will keep you strong and confident.

On the other hand, habits of ungratefulness, lying, stealing, unfairness, unkindness, hatred, anger, non forgiveness, laziness, not being considerate of others, faithlessness, and hopelessness will defeat you and make you a loser.

Virtues and principles determine the kind of habits we form.

Our sense of life purpose determines our habits (good or bad).

THE LAW OF THE HANDSHAKE

The first few seconds of body language are frequently all the communication one may have with the most important people in your future. First impressions count greatly in business and other meaningful life relationships.

The foundation of the hand shake is the show of "no harm intended" (NHI) and is usually extended man to man. The extended hand offers more than NHI; it offers acceptance that leads to contracts and friendships. With body square, face to face and a pleasant countenance, a man/woman offers, "Peace, NHI," when he/she extends a hand.

Some American Indians used the greeting of, "How!" with the fighting hand raised palm forward to show no weapon in hand and the NHI attitude, while providing a friendly face and eye contact. American military personnel greet (or salute) with the right hand palm down 45 degrees, fingers joined, and index finger at the bill of the hat, or eye brow to state recognition of the chain of command. The NHI British military tradition is to bring the right hand palm forward to the right side of the head with a click of the heels. An American man salutes a lady by touching the brim of his hat, or tipping his hat, with a nod and smile.

Take advantage of offering your hand first with the extension of a simultaneous verbal greeting, such as, "Hello, my name is Thomas, Tom Jones, I'm here with the Texas Cattle Brokers, and you are who, Sir/Ms.?" Offering your name first allows you to concentrate on hearing/learning the other person's name. When he/she offers his/her name, use the name in some way, such as: "Are you a cattleman, Mr./Mrs. Overtake?" The reply may be, "Call me Henry(etta)." "All right, Henry(eta), what do you expect the price of beef to be ... ?"

Gentlemen! If you are greeting a person in authority, or a lady, do not extend your hand first. Why? Because ladies and superiors have the choice whether to be touched. Also, this allows the superior and/or a lady to be gracious and extend the hand salutation. Hand greeting with a lady is a slight hand pressure and no shake.

Ladies have the same opportunity as a man to approach a man and introduce herself with a hand greeting. A lady approaching another woman is wise to follow the same rule regarding superiors.

(James R. Lathrop, Lieutenant Colonel, Army, Retired)

THE LAW OF HAPPINESS

Happiness is the result of wise choices.

Everyone seeks happiness as if it were a right.

Happiness is not found in people, things, money, places, achievements, popularity, or power.

Happiness is not the same as fulfillment.

Happiness is a clear conscience and a noble life purpose.

Happiness is usually elusive; at best it is momentary.

People were not created or designed to be happy. They were designed to reflect goodness, kindness, virtue, and courage. Such people usually ARE happy!

Happy people are those who are able to live with purpose in spite of negative circumstances.

Happy people are directed by noble life purpose rather than other people.

Happiness is obtained through serving others in need.

People live happily while pursuing a noble life purpose.

THE LAW OF HEADLIGHTS

He who overruns his headlights collects critters in his grill!

Don't overrun your headlights while pursuing adulthood!

Wise people go along life's roads at speeds appropriate for conditions during sunny days, rainy nights, or snow storms.

A heavy foot on the pedal causes you to overrun the probing distance of your head lights, prohibiting you from avoiding collisions.

Don't rush through life as if you needed to speed through teenage training in preparation for adult responsibilities.

Put a throttle on your curiosity, desire for freedom and attraction to the opposite gender, otherwise you may overrun your maturity headlights ... and likely collect a lot of critters (consequences).

Headlights are principles, values and virtues which guide not only where you travel, but how fast you get there without collecting critters in your grill.

Sometimes the best policy is not to pursue goals at night. Daylight is usually best and safest to travel life's road. Eagles fly in the sunlight and rest at night—good advice!

THE LAW OF THE HEART

Out of the heart come the issues of life.

The human heart beats about once every second (when resting).

The heart gallops when exercised or excited by passion or anger.

The heart is the resting place for affection and love. The heart is a reservoir for passion and anger.

The human symbol for love is a heart pierced by an arrow [From the mythical Greek god of love "Cupid."]

The affections you allow to enter your heart determine your destiny.

Human hearts abide in three places: 1) the body; 2) the soul; 3) the spirit.

Be careful to whom you "give your heart"; your life will follow along behind. You go where your heart leads you.

(See Figure 14)

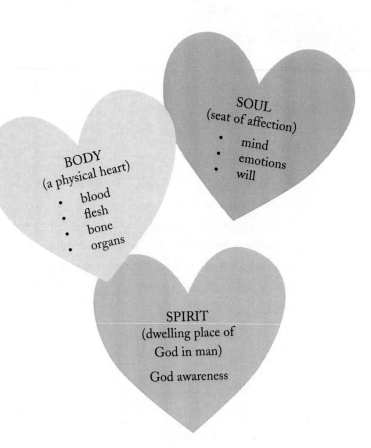

Figure 14

THE LAW OF HELPING OTHERS

People who help others help themselves.

Achievers are people who see tasks that need to be done, and do them regardless of who gets the credit.

Help others in need and let the credit fall anywhere it lands—you will come out on top.

H   *Hear what they say,*

E   *Envision their dream,*

L   *Let them try,*

P   *Provide things they need to succeed.*

O   *Offer assistance,*

T   *Train them to succeed,*

H   *Head them in the right direction,*

E   *Erase their mistakes,*

R   *Reach out when they are in need,*

S   *Say "Well done" for completed tasks.*

THE LAW OF HONESTY

Honesty brings out your best qualities and character.

Integrity is honesty to do what you should do and do what you say you will do.

Honesty keeps the conscience clear, which gives you confidence to be all you can be.

Dishonesty damages credibility.

Dishonesty is cowardly; fear of consequences of choices tempts us to modify truth to protect ourselves.

Dishonesty is expressed as:

- Gossip (hurt others)
- Flattery (impress others)
- Lies (deceive others)
- Theft (rob others)
- Laziness (stealing time)
- Cheating (rob self)

Honest men keep their jobs. Dishonest men are fired.

THE LAW OF HOPE

Hope for a better tomorrow carries us past oppressive conditions today.

Hope is but a childish fantasy until definitive steps are taken to reach a definite goal.

Hope is confidence of the soul (mind, will, emotions) that the steps that I am taking today will lead me toward a goal.

Hope is a vital ingredient of life. Without hope, life stagnates.

Hope deferred makes the heart sad.

Hope and faith are siblings.

Hope is kept alive by integrity.

Purpose never to destroy another person's hope.

People can usually make it through tough times with hope.

People take courage when supported by at least one other person who offers hope.

People hope for success when they bond with at least one person who cares.

"Hopeless" people tend to recover when supported by people who instill hope.

Daily accountability to someone virtuous helps keep us focused on choices and consequences that either inspire or destroy hope.

THE LAW OF
HORMONES AND LIFE PURPOSE

Hormones drive impulses necessary for survival and replenishing of families.

Hormones that affect sexual desires are chemicals activated during three basic stages of life:

- Six year molars (ready for structured learning and organized physical activity such as sports, games, etc.).

- Twelve year molars (ready for cognitive exercise, beginning of puberty/capable of physical reproduction)

- The change of life (decrease in child bearing or reproductive ability/beginning of training others in wisdom).

Hormones drive responses to stimulation of senses (sight, touch, smell, sound, etc.).

Life purpose guides expression of hormone impulses.

Raging hormones at puberty (12 year molars) can get out of control without moral restraint and focus on noble character. Focus on character and noble life purpose strengthen a person's ability to suppress raging hormones and sexual stimulation.

A teenager will be controlled by hormone urges unless restrained by a noble life purpose which protects the virtues of other people.

Temptation to express hormonal urges to reproduce life is a product of creation/design for married men and women.

Man is designed to desire woman (and vice versa) within a covenant of marriage that can provide for and protect children.

Sex as recreation outside of marriage violates the virtues and integrity of both persons, thus is not natural as designed.

Hormones out of control lead to consequences that control our future choices.

Children born of sexual acts outside of marriage usually face life without the protection and provision of a Dad who loves his wife.

Adolescents are wise to abstain from hormonal expression until the "act of marriage" is legitimate (noble).

THE LAW OF
HUMAN COMPOSITION

Humans consist of interdependent components:

- body

- soul

- spirit

These interdependent components are foundational to lifestyle choices and achievement:

- each impacts and is impacted by the others

- the body is the gate to the soul; the soul is the gate to the spirit; the spirit is the gate to destiny.

A person is successful only as he/she lives in such a way that life choices nurture body, soul, and spirit.

A person who abuses the body of another person damages his/her own soul and spirit.

A person is never complete without attention to body, soul and spirit.

(See Figure 15)

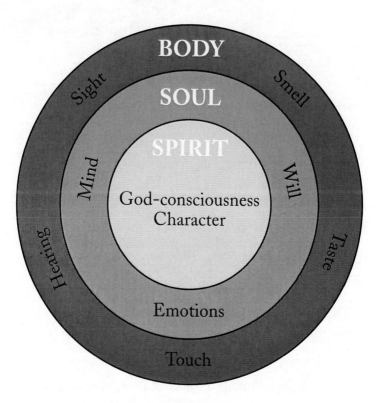

Figure 15

THE LAW OF HUMILITY

Humble people are meek (submissive to authority); therefore, they are strong and capable of performing their life missions.

Strong character and confidence to be valiant and noble are based in humbleness (humility).

People who live to meet the needs of others are characterized by humility.

Every noble cause is championed by humble people.

Humility is to:

- Pick up trash on the sidewalk

- Say "I'm sorry" for rudeness

- Listen when you really want to talk

- Give honor or credit to someone else

- Help a friend or neighbor (when you had rather be elsewhere)

- Receive correction and instruction without anger or resentment.

THE LAW OF HYGIENE

Eagles fly high because they practice daily hygiene. They clean their wings, beaks, and talons of dirt, food, and debris.

That is good advice for youth, too—to keep the mouth, hands, feet, armpits, and private areas clean.

Odor emitting from the body, dirt under the fingernails, and food between the teeth can cost a man employment or a happy marriage.

Wise is the young man who inspects his body before bounding out the door: hair combed, teeth brushed, hands washed, whiskers shaved, and torso showered. [Fresh socks and underwear and deodorant help keep friends.]

Of most importance is a clean heart at the start of each day. No abuse toward others, no bitterness, anger, or strife should be carried out the door. Eagles leave the "junk" behind when they spread their wings to soar.

A daily inspection of the mind is recommended to clean out toxic thoughts that weigh down the body, soul, and spirit. Clean out bitterness, anger, lust, envy, strife, and jealousy. Set your mind on things that are true, good, just, pure, and virtuous. A man free of toxic "stuff" and focused on lofty dreams will soar high!

THE LAW OF IGNORANCE

We don't know what we don't know. Just because we know something better than someone else knows something doesn't make us smarter than the other person.

Youth falsely presume to be of superior intelligence simply because they were taught to text message, email, operate an iPod, surf the Internet, or adjust a DVD player. Their technical skill to send or receive information is not a sign of superior intelligence. *It only reflects the ability to entertain oneself with gadgets created by intelligent people.*

Knowledge about something created by others is the lowest of the three levels of intelligence. Understanding is the second level. Wisdom is the highest level of human "smartness."

Wise people are not ignorant, nor are ignorant people wise or smart. Wise people know that they don't know. Ignorant people think they know. To be wise is to be smart. To presume that you are smarter than others when you are not wise is ignorance.

People who fail to learn wisdom remain ignorant failures.

THE LAW OF
INCREMENTAL AWARENESS

Each experience awakens old memories, reinforces habits or breaks open new awareness about life.

Some "little" information or acts can be "huge" events that close or open doors of opportunity for success or failure.

Each subsequent act, thought, or habit is an incremental experience that closes or opens the "doors" of life opportunities.

Events are door openers or closers that move us incrementally toward or away from our dreams, goals, purpose.

Be aware of the thoughts, ideas or suggestions you allow to rest in your soul; they will act upon your will to influence your habits (lifestyle).

(See Figure 16)

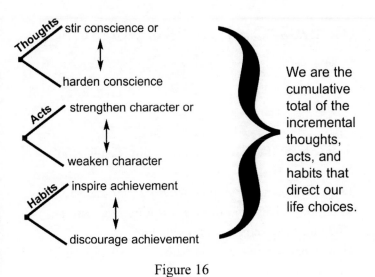

Figure 16

THE LAW OF JOB PROMOTION

If you are not on track to earn a promotion, you will not advance.

Promotion comes from productivity and initiative.

Intentions, plans, and desires for promotion cannot replace actual achievement and production.

Hard work, extra effort, initiative, punctuality, and skills bring promotion.

Accomplishments earn promotion.

Initiative to act on intentions determines promotion.

Promotion comes from productivity that makes an employee valuable.

Every task (assignment) is an opportunity to learn a new skill or insight.

Promotion comes from giving a person (boss) what you are paid to accomplish.

Job security rests in your commitment to meet the needs of the employer.

You will be promoted as you make yourself necessary to the mission of your employer.

THE LAW OF THE LADDER

Successful people who attain goals usually help others who aspire to attain their goals.

Everyone desires to be successful, to reach a goal in life. A goal is reached one step at a time.

Steps are often disguised as obstacles, when in reality they are necessary experiences that strengthen and equip us for more difficult tasks we will face in our quest to reach a goal.

People who aspire to a goal recognize the assistance of other people who reach down to pull up others, and those who extend arms to push others upward and over obstacles.

By pushing those ahead of us and pulling those behind us, we all move toward attainment of our goals.

People who try to shove others off the ladder usually fail to reach the top.

(See Figure 17)

Figure 17

THE LAW OF LEADERSHIP

Leadership is influence.

The secret of leadership is integrity and the ability to inspire others to fulfill a cause (purpose).

Leaders live with a sense of destiny or purpose that compels action to reach goals.

Leadership is not position or authority over other people; it is the ability to influence and guide others to complete personal, group, or corporate goals.

Leaders rise to the level of the need regardless of their employment position in the organization or company.

Leaders solve problems and inspire other people to achieve goals.

THE LAW OF LIFE OPTIONS

You have a right to select available options that are within your control.

Identify practices and habits in your life that must change in order to reduce problems and their negative effects on you.

Select an option in your lifestyle or associates that must change in order to remove the problem, or change it into a positive asset.

People who live with purpose, integrity, virtue, and positive sense of destiny retain options for relationships and employment.

A life marked by toxic activities has few options other than grief, poverty, incarceration, fear and broken dreams.

Life options are restricted or created by our character.

THE LAW OF LINES

Everyone faces situations in which lines must be drawn—to step over or stand behind.

Lines are drawn in the soul (mind, will, emotions), and when based on morals, virtues, and principles, enable a person to act with integrity.

Character based on morals and virtues enables a person to face "lines" in life with confidence to act courageously when faced with temptations to act selfishly or cowardly.

Col. Travis drew a line in the sand at the Alamo and challenged his men to step over the line if they were willing to defend freedom unto death.

Temptations to do wrong or opportunities to act with moral courage are always set off with a "line" of decision.

Lines drawn privately in the mind will be in place publicly to apply during relationship interaction, at work, or in battle.

THE LAW OF LISTENING

Wisdom comes by hearing/listening.

God gave us two ears and one mouth so we would listen twice as much as we speak.

What goes into your ears (words, music) goes into your soul (mind, will, emotions).

What goes into your soul determines your habits and desires (what you want in life). Lifestyle habits determine your destiny.

Who you listen to builds your desires (wants) and/or your dislikes for people, places, and principles.

Listening is the way people shape habits, desires, and values:

- Words in media (movies, television, the news, talk shows, etc.)

- Words in songs (lyrics can influence you toward a certain lifestyle)

- Words from/with peers

Listen to your thoughts. Are they of joy, peace, love, contentment, kindness and hope, or are they of depression, anger, lust, hopelessness, or rebellion?

Wise listeners tune into words that are true, pure, lovely, just, and honest.

Wise people walk away or cover their ears when toxic words are voiced.

THE LAW OF LITTLE CHOICES

Big things are made of many little things.

A messed up life is the accumulation of little toxic thoughts or negative choices and experiences done habitually until they define a life.

LITTLE THINGS MEAN A LOT!

The road to success is paved with positive little choices made consistently. [Go to bed early, wake up early, dress quickly and appropriately, make your bed, hang up your clothes, eat nutritiously at least two meals daily with family, avoid toxic energy drains.]

STOP ONE BAD HABIT TODAY;
START ONE GOOD HABIT TODAY ...

... then move on by dropping other bad habits, while adding good habits until, little by little, you are a noble person.

Resisting a little bad habit today strengthens you to resist a bigger bad habit tomorrow.

People who are too big to help others are too little for big jobs.

You are defined by your little choices.

LITTLE THINGS

Little drops of water,
little grains of sand,
make the mighty ocean
and the pleasant land.

And the little moments,
humble though they be,
make the mighty ages
of eternity.

Little deeds of kindness,
little words of love,
make our earth an Eden,
like the heav'n above.

So our little errors
lead the soul away,
from the paths of virtue
into sin to stray.

Little seeds of mercy
sown by youthful hands,
grow to bless the nations
far in heathen lands.

Glory then for ever
be to God on high,
beautiful and loving,
to Him I shall draw nigh.

(Julia Carney, 1845)

THE LAW OF LOVE

Mankind was created to love and be loved. A man or woman who does not love God will "love" self (narcissism/self love) or pleasure (Hedonism/love of pleasure) in an effort to fill the void created to be fulfilled by God.

Love is meeting the needs (body, soul and spirit) of another person without expecting anything in return/exchange. True love is unity of soul, spirit, and body—not just two bodies in intimacy.

"I love you" may simply mean, "I like your body and face … and want to touch you."

A boy stimulated by sight (of a girl's body) may say, "I love you," when he actually means, "I want your body for my pleasure." Girls are stimulated by touch and words; therefore can be vulnerable to the "I love you" trap.

Boys interpret a girl's touch and exposed body as invitations to intimacy ("making love"). A boy who pressures a girl for intimacy before marriage does not love her; his lust is not based on love because it puts the girl at risk of a bruised life (guilt, loss of purity, STD, pregnancy).

Girls think "true love" when the guy says, "I love you." She embraces (allows touch in private areas) because she hopes/thinks her submission to his lust will lead to true love and happiness while giving her an escape from mental or physical (home) misery, neglect or abuse (real or perceived).

The probable result of "fake love" is pregnancy and/or STDs and disappointment in a series of broken relationships that leave teens fragmented and confused—controlled by toxic memories and broken dreams. Every time you "make love" (sexual intimacy), you give away part of your soul; eventually, when you marry, you are able to give to your spouse only a part of the original you, and your spouse ends up mentally competing with all of your previous partners ("lovers"). That is not fair to either party. That is why many marriages fall apart … too many partners. A boy cannot meet a girl's needs until the boy becomes a mature and discerning man who knows a girl's needs (body, soul, and spirit) and knows how to meet those needs as a legitimate husband. If a person does not know how to meet your needs, he/she does not love you (regardless of what he/she says).

A woman (girl) needs security as much as she needs affection (touch and words). Her security is based on a man's positive virtues, commitment, integrity, responsibility, compassion, leadership and love (meeting her needs).

A girl without the protective care of her father is vulnerable to predators who offer or demand sexual favors. A man is fulfilled only as he assumes responsibility to meet the needs of other people—to provide security for those he loves. He cannot be a "true lover" until he has knowledge, understanding, and wisdom about, and meets the needs of his wife.

Regardless of the past, today is a new beginning in your pursuit of "true love." Purpose to reject "false lovers" while you wait for a "real lover" … someone who cherishes and protects your body, soul, and spirit in marriage.

- Love is a gift from God's heart to mankind.

- Love is not lust—though often misapplied by people who say, "let's make love."

- Love cannot be "made."

- Love is the product of virtue.

- Love meets another person's needs without expecting anything in return.

- Lust takes from a person (purity, worth, health, virtue, peace of mind).

- Love between a man and woman is appropriately expressed physically in the "act of marriage."

- True "lovers" wait (suppress sexual desires) until marriage.

THE LAW OF LUST

Sexual lust grips the soul and drives it to commit abusive acts.

Lust begins in the soul (mind, will, emotions) and compels expression.

Lust enters the soul through the senses (eyes, ears, touch, taste, smell).

Lust expresses itself in a quest for power, gratification, and abuse, often in the form of rape or homosexuality.

Lust is a constant force, but has only a temporary, false satisfaction.

The consequence of lust is expressed in acts against other people.

Lust eventually results in emotional depression for both the abused and the abuser. People abused by acts of lust feel victimized and cheated—as if something precious (dignity) has been stolen, and that they have been made "cheap" and "unworthy" of life.

Lust = violence against self and others. Lust = depression.

Depression is "driven" out of the soul only by virtue and righteousness "fed" through the senses. Anti-depressant (drug) prescriptions cannot cure depressions; they only suppress depression.

The only way to avoid the negative consequences of lust is to feed the soul with virtuous "matter" while protecting the soul from lustful stimulation through the five senses.

The only cure for lust is a life committed to virtue and chastity.

THE LAW OF THE "LY'S"

Dream	Daring*ly!*
Think	Nob*ly!*
Live	Virtuous*ly!*
Help	Generous*ly!*
Plan	Careful*ly!*
Fail	Optimistical*ly!*
Work	Diligent*ly!*
Fellowship	Discreet*ly!*
Worship	Reverent*ly!*
Speak	Kind*ly!*
Listen	Attentive*ly!*
Read	Selective*ly!*
Pray	Humb*ly!*
Sleep	Peaceful*ly!*
Eat	Nutritious*ly!*
Exercise	Regular*ly!*
Invest	Proportional*ly!*
Defend	Courageous*ly!*
Dress	Modest*ly!*
Meditate	Quiet*ly!*
Obey	Gracious*ly!*
Volunteer	Unselfish*ly!*

THE LAW OF MEANING

The meaning of your life is made known only when you put eternity in the equation. A survey of college students revealed that they wanted to know the meaning of life. Sixteen percent said, "to make money." Seventy-six percent said, "to know what life is about" such as, "Where did I come from?," "Why am I here?," "Where am I going?"

Man exists in a closed system (earth), but he has a destiny beyond life on earth (eternity).

Eternity is in the heart of every person. Without a sense of eternity, the present makes little sense.

Life has no meaning for people who believe they are the result of a cosmic accident. That's why the U.S. Congress established the national motto, "In God We Trust"—because all else is futile and meaningless and hopeless.

THE LAW OF
MEASURED DIFFERENCE

The difference between first and second place is small. People who become winners and succeed in life or "get the job," are those who demonstrate a measurable difference in training, skill, attitude, and appearance.

Successful people march to a different drum beat than the crowd. Being different is neither good nor bad; the difference is application of good or bad values and motives. A well dressed, polite, and articulate person driven by purpose based on moral values is different—and likely to succeed.

People who follow the crowd's attire, attitude, and activities are different than leaders and entrepreneurs who make a difference for their country. Rebellious, arrogant people who say, "I want to be different" usually hang out with "look-alikes."

If you want to make a measurable difference in society, let your difference be in strong moral character, integrity, and a noble life purpose.

THE LAW OF THE MIND

The mind is a battle ground of thoughts and feelings stored in two hemispheres of the brain. Your soul (mind, will, emotions) was designed to experience virtuous love, positive thinking, to be stable, and have power over toxic or negative emotions.

Toxic thoughts are based in a cluttered conscience/mind caused by such negative thinking/experiences as anger, bitterness, guilt, fear, pornography, shame, sorrow, and trauma.

Your mind is one third of the soul (mind, will, emotions). It is the processing station of all data received through your senses (touch, taste, smell, hearing, sight) and developer of your spirit (home of your conscience and where character determines your life style).

The mind consists of two hemispheres (right: emotions/feelings and left: data filing and organization). Mind clutter "jams" the circuits that process the electrical and chemical transmitters between the two hemispheres, causing discouragement, depression, negative choices, and distractions from goals and responsibilities.

Negative life choices will continue to dominate the mind until it is detoxified by positive (new) input received through the senses.

The mind is detoxified/uncluttered by "washing" and reprogramming it with selective, positive input and experiences through choices such as forgiving people who have been abusive, engaging in wholesome laughter, learning wisdom, associating with "uncluttered" people/ peers, choosing wholesome music and activities... and avoiding "toxic" people and experiences (drugs, alcohol, occult, lust, dares to steal, lie, abuse).

Your mind is healthy only to the extent that you "mind" your manners and live with a clear conscience! (See Figure 18)

Figure 18

THE LAW OF MIND MAPPING

We attain or obtain that which we first visualize in our soul (mind, will, emotions).

We arrive at wherever we are going in our thoughts.

We move toward a place, condition, or goal first visualized in the mind.

Maps are designed to help us get from "here" to "there."

People who follow maps arrive at their destination with minimum expenses of time and resources.

People who create a mind map of their dreams or goals are able to focus on the best way to get from "here" to "there."

Mind maps that lead our thoughts toward goals include photos of scenes, vehicles, facilities, awards, etc.

Every noble dream is first mapped in the mind.

THE LAW OF MONEY

Employers pay money to productive workers.

Honorable work is noble.

Work earns money and self-respect.

Money determines lifestyle.

The "10–10–80" formula is stabilizing to a productive lifestyle:

- earn = 100%

- charity/tithe/offering = 10%

- save = 10%

- live on (pay bills/expenses/fun) = 80%

People are paid money in exchange for labor that produces profit.

Avoid debt: live on your earned money (not credit).

Invest in self-improvement to enhance career options that increase your monetary value:

- study (skill training) programs

- attend seminars/conferences

- complete college courses

- read beneficial/positive books

A good salary (income of money) is good, but remember, possessions do not reflect success.

Money earned rightfully gives options of the lifestyle you practice: the more money you earn, the more lifestyle options you have.

People are not employed because they need a job; they earn wages for productive labor exchanged for money.

THE LAW OF
MORAL RELEVANCE

Morals originate in the mind of man or God.

All societies are based on morals, virtues, and values.

Every person/culture (group of people) decides which morals to follow.

All personal or cultural decisions are based on moral values.

One of the highest compliments a man can receive is the statement, "I feel safe around you because you are a man of good morals."

LIFE IS BASED ON ABSOLUTES:

Humans reproduce humans. Cows reproduce cows. Birds are hatched from eggs. The sun heats the earth. All snowflakes are unique. Trees require oxygen. All creatures die. Love is real. Prayers affect outcomes. Virtues enhance quality of life. Electricity can kill you. People die from diseases. Crops require water. Volcanoes are predictable but not preventable. DNA is unique.

MORAL ABSOLUTES ARE EVIDENT IN AMERICAN CULTURE:

People who rob and steal face punishment. Rapists and pedophiles are identified as harmful to children and women. Personal privacy is protected. Freedom to pursue happiness is sacred. Religious freedom is central to American culture. A man or woman who abandons his/her spouse/children is not respected. Infidelity (adultery/cheating on a spouse) destroys marriages and families.

AMERICA IS FOUNDED ON TRADITIONAL MORAL VALUES:

The Constitutional Bill of Rights defines American values. Husbands and wives should be faithful to one another. The national motto is "In God We Trust." Public officials are expected to be honest and trustworthy. Parents have the right to decide who educates their children. Judges are expected to punish criminals. Employees are expected to be honest, hard working, and helpful to the employer so a profit can be made, the business become successful, and the employee retain his job, receive a paycheck, and earn promotions!

THE LAW OF MORE

The more virtue we accumulate in life, the "more" we create room for success.

"More" can be counted in possessions, insight, or responsibilities.

People who are "full of themselves" have no room for others or "more" in life.

People who express gratitude for what they have seem to get "more" in life than people who have "less" in life.

People who have "less" and do not work to get "more" lose the "less."

Expressing gratitude for what you do have creates room for more of what you want or need to be fulfilled or to reach your goals.

To whom much is given, much is required. People who get "more" have "more" (ability) to take care of "more."

Take care of and express gratitude for what you have and you earn the right, privilege, and responsibility of taking care of "more."

THE LAW OF
MORNING PREPARATION

A person walks daily in the path for which he/she prepares in thoughts upon awakening.

As a person thinks in the morning, so he/she is throughout the day.

Morning thoughts harbored get moored to the afternoon wharf.

A morning *thought* entertained daily
becomes an evening *desire;*
A desire repeated becomes a *habit;*
A habit sustained forms *character;*
Character determines *destiny!*

Wise people recognize toxic thoughts (which if not suppressed) lead to acts that could impede a great destiny, then such people deliberately verbalize denouncement of such negative thoughts, and vocalize the opposite positive thought as the desire of the heart—then make daily choices based on the vocalized positive desire. Their positive, noble thoughts each morning prepare the path to be walked that day.

THE LAW OF
MOTIVATIONAL TEMPERMENT

Every person has a temperament composition that motivates decisions about goals, careers, and relationships.

Every temperament has strengths and weaknesses that benefit or restrict achievements.

Most people are dominant in one of four temperaments.

Our dominant temperament tends to determine our lifestyle.

Wise people cultivate their dominant strengths and harness their temperament weaknesses.

Your motivational DNA (temperament) "drives" your mind, will, and emotions in social relationships, career, and lifestyle.

(See Figure 19)

CHOLERIC	SANGUINE
• ruler (bossy) • exact (intolerant) • projects (no frills)	• optimistic/energetic • fun/needs attention • careless/lack commitment
PHLEGMATIC	MELANCHOLY
• peacemaker (compromises) • laid-back (follower) "whatever" mentality	• idealist/perfectionist • serious (depressed) • creative (organized) • introvert/loner

CHOLERIC	SANGUINE
• likes structure/ and systems • organization • purpose/goals • courageous • bold/"frank" • entrepreneurial	• likes drama • salesman/actor/ performer • people oriented • motivating • humorous/joking • "shallow"/"fake"

aspects
of each
temperment
style

PHLEGMATIC	MELANCHOLY
• calming • team oriented • practical • steady/stable • dry humor • reliable • unpretentious	• strategist • writer/artist • scholar/inventor • thinker/planner • philosopher • "mad genius" • "deep" person

Figure 19

THE LAW OF MULTIPLE "A'S"

Success in life rests on how well we manage the A's.

	(Positive)	(Negative)
ATTITUDE (how we see life)	life is opportunity	life is unfair (victim)
ASSOCIATES (friends we select)	build us up	hamper us
ATTENDENCE (school/job)	on time	absent/late
ACADEMIC (school assignments)	complete	neglect/fail
ASPIRATIONS (life dreams)	noble	degrading
ASSIGNMENTS (everyday tasks)	fulfill	avoid/incomplete
ATTIRE (how we dress)	appropriate	careless

APPETITE (what we eat/desire)	you control it	it controls you
ACHIEVEMENT (accomplishments)	improve self	weaken potential
ADULTS (around us)	role models	excuses for failure
AFFIRMATIONS (praise/criticism)	raise dreams	lower dreams/ goals

THE LAW OF THE NECKTIE

Every man should know how to tie and wear a necktie. To do so opens doors of opportunity for relationships and careers. To be ignorant about neckties is to be handicapped in your pursuit of your dream.

Step 1: Start with the wide end of the tie on your right and extend it a foot (12 inches) below the narrow end.

Step 2: Cross the wide end over the narrow end and bring it up through the loop.

Step 3: Cross the wide end over the narrow end and bring it up through the loop.

Step 4: Put the wide end down through the loop and around across the narrow end (as shown).

Step 5: Turn the wide end up through the loop.

Step 6: Finish by slipping the wide end down through the knot in front. Tighten and draw up snugly to the collar.

(See Figure 20)

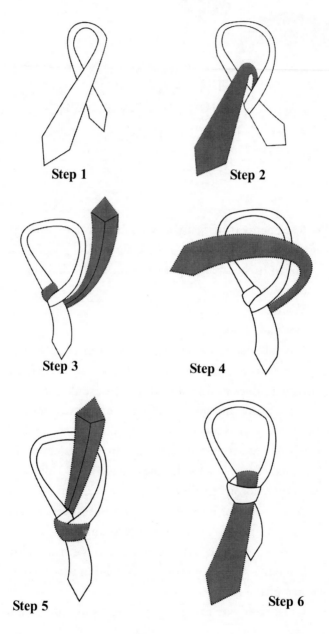

Figure 20

THE LAW OF
NEGATIVE ENERGY DRAINS
AND POSITIVE BLESSINGS

We lose energy (spiritually, physically, mentally) through negative (toxic) actions by us or against us.

Harsh (toxic) words against us (or by us) drain emotional energy.

Words of encouragement (from us or to us) raise our emotions and hopes.

Lustful acts by us or against us drain energy from our bodies, souls, and spirits. Sexual abstinence before marriage enables positive health in body, soul, and spirit.

Kind words and positive affirmations of worth by us or toward us lift souls (mind, will, emotions) (ours and theirs). Many patients in hospitals are victims of toxic, emotional energy drains that negatively impact physical health (psychosomatic illness).

Any encounter or expression that raises fear, sorrow or regret is a negative (toxic) energy drain.

A clear conscience is a prerequisite to positive health.

"God bless you" is a positive affirmation that encourages people.

Curse words are toxic, negative expressions that drain dignity.

Meeting the needs of others without expecting anything in return is an expression of love—a blessing.

Love blesses; it never drains (takes away) energy.

What we hear, see, and experience either drains or enhances our energy in body, soul, and spirit.

Energy drains from us as we experience anger, criticism, rejection, abuse, poor nutrition, and lack of sleep or exercise.

Positive intake equals energy supply. Negative intake equals negative drain.

Intake in the body, soul, or spirit, equals our output… building or tearing down potential achievements.

Words of affirmation build energy. Criticism drains energy. Intake in body, soul, and spirit, equals our output… building or tearing down potential achievements.

We tend to attract positive or negative energy according to the kind of people we think we are. "As we think, so we are."

What we believe about our worth affects how and where our energy level is supplied. How we dress, speak, and listen reflects/affects our energy levels in body, soul, and spirit.

People who have healthy energy levels know who and what to avoid, and how and where to gather positive energy.

Sources of positive or negative intake:

- Associates
- Chemical substances (family, peers, others)
- Curses/Blessings (negative or positive family legacy)

- Media
- Traditions
- Literature
- Exercise
- Activities
- Thoughts and reflections
- Lyrics (music)
- Food habits

THE LAW OF NOBLE CAUSES

Focus on a noble cause tends to carry a person past temptations and acceptance of mediocrity.

Vignettes of noble persons instill a sense of identity with nobleness: George Washington, Abraham Lincoln, David Livingston, Gladys Alyward, Tom Landry, William Booth, Mother Teresa, and other history makers.

Identification with a noble cause brings out the "best" in youth. The purpose-driven life is always tied to a noble cause that helps humanity.

Extra-curricular activities expand life options. The higher we operate in the Pyramid of Life, the more likely we are to be fulfilled with a noble sense of life purpose, and less likely to forfeit our dreams.

(See Figure 21)

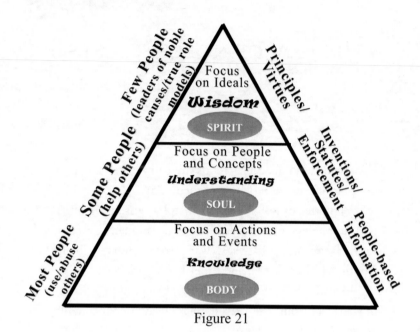

Figure 21

THE LAW OF OPPORTUNITY

Successful people seize opportunities when they appear.

Character and preparation equip one to take advantage of opportunities.

People who live with a dream are constantly alert to take advantage of sudden opportunities.

Sudden opportunities often require risky decisions to give up comfort and safety to pursue a dream.

An opportunity is usually a step from a comfort zone to an unknown position necessary to reach a dream.

People who live primarily to satisfy physical desires seldom recognize opportunities for achieving a better tomorrow.

Opportunities are usually cloaked in work or effort to complete a task or assignment that is actually another step toward achieving a dream.

Wise people recognize and take advantage of opportunities when they appear.

THE LAW OF ORDERLY LIVING

Successful people follow a daily routine regarding basic orderliness.

WISE YOUTH LEARN TO DO THE FOLLOWING DAILY:

AT HOME

1. Get up promptly at a set time each morning
2. Make bed before leaving their room
3. Line up shoes under bed or in closet before sleep
4. Hang or fold clothes in specified places
5. Dress appropriately for duties
6. Eat at least one meal with family
7. Read and/or discuss a wholesome topic with parents before going to sleep (before 9:00 p.m.)
8. Say to parents, "I love you."

AT SCHOOL

1. Sign in/out promptly
2. Keep desk/office orderly
3. Put books/notebooks in proper places
4. Place personal items as directed
5. Dress appropriately for learning
6. Eat nutritious food at school
7. Read and complete academics before leaving school
8. Say to staff, "Thank you."

THE LAW OF
ORPHANS AND WIDOWS

Fatherless youth are provided special status and opportunities with God and the United States of America.

- The Northwest Ordinance of 1787 established that local governments were to set aside land and money to take care of orphans and widows.

- "True and undefiled religion is to take care of fatherless youth and widows." (Ref. James 1:27)

- "A child forsaken by his father and mother is protected by the Lord." (Ref. Psalms 27:10)

- "Defend the fatherless, make provisions for the widow." (Ref. Isaiah 1:17)

- God called leaders wicked who did not "defend orphans or pay attention to the conditions of widows" (Ref. Isaiah 1:23)

The hurt and pain of fatherlessness is often motivation to become the kind of person the father should have been.

Fatherless youth who are trained to practice the national motto (In God We Trust) become wise, noble, and courageous because they willingly place themselves under the wings of virtuous protection and guidance. (Ref. Psalms 25)

Adults who serve as umbrellas for protection for fatherless youth are blessed.

THE LAW OF OTHERS

What you think about yourself affects how you think about and treat other people.

"Me, Myself, and I" leaves no room for joy in others.

Happiness is in direct proportion to how we relate to and serve/help others.

Hedonism = lover of self-pleasure ("I love pleasure, even at the expense of others").

Narcissism = lover of self ("I love me too much to love others").

"Self-made men" is a myth; we all stand on the shoulders of others to look at our past, present and future.

Others around us shape/influence who we are becoming.

"Do I like the kind of persons my peers are becoming by participating in my lifestyle?"

"Do my choices help or hinder others who need the kind of help I need?"

Every social encounter should benefit others.

Other people should benefit from our presence.

We should never damage the virtue of others by our influence or presence.

THE LAW OF
OUR THOUGHT WORLD

We perceive the world to be as we live it (our experiences, our peers, our family, our relatives, our neighbors, our literature, our music, T.V.).

We remain as "our world" until we change our perception about who we think we are.

As a person thinks, so is he. We can think our world into becoming the real world.

Knowledge increases thinking power, but good thinking is based on wisdom.

Wisdom is living as a person guided by thoughts of virtue, principles, goodness, grace, kindness, courage, truth, compassion, integrity.

As we think on these things, our world enlarges and "things change."

If you always do what your world has always done, your world will always be what it has always been.

We don't know what we don't know about the world.

We live in a big world, yet "our world" is small and is changed by small thoughts, ideas, choices, or experiences.

We change here a little and there a little, line upon line, precept upon precept.

Wise people think carefully about daily choices that frame their world.

Make your mind think wisely; it is a choice.

THE LAW OF PASSION

Passion is the inner drive of the soul (mind, will, emotions) to fulfill or complete objectives.

Passion is driven by thoughts focused on an objective. Those thoughts drive your life choices.

Your life choices (passions) are controlled by your virtues, values, and principles.

Your thoughts, passions, and life choices are rooted in who you are.

Your passions control you. If your thoughts are only on passionate physical relationships, your life choices will be at the physical level of passion.

If your thoughts are toward wisdom, knowledge, and understanding of information and ideas, your passions will be noble, good, joyful.

You control your passions by taking command of your thoughts—making them focus on noble dreams, goals, and objectives.

A wise person avoids people and places where passion could overrule virtues and chastity.

Sadly, most people are driven by passion to experience physical pleasure. Thus, negative life experiences are repeated day after day, month after month, generation after generation.

Your lifestyle changes as you direct your thoughts away from physical passions and toward noble ideals that command your brain to seek new virtues, principles, and moral values with which to change your life and the world.

THE LAW OF PEOPLE

Wisely choose the people who influence you.

We can't avoid contact with people, but we can choose the kind of people who affect us.

Achievements or failures are often based on the people we know. Someone once said, "The world would be a great place to live if we just didn't have to get along with people."

We are blessed or cursed by people.

Some people are "bridge" people who connect us to opportunities or resources. Some people are "hinge" people whose council or influence turns us (like a hinge) from one direction to another; they change our focus.

Our fulfillment in life is based on how we are a blessing (not a curse) to people.

THE LAW OF
PERCENTAGES OF ACCOUNTABILITY

Conflict is avoided or resolved in direct proportion to acceptance of personal accountability for choices and responses.

The more percentage of responsibility I take for causing conflict or an unfulfilled assignment, the more likely the issue will be resolved.

Each participating person takes responsibility for his percentage of accountability in the conflict, then acts responsibly to bring about resolution:

- admit your percentage of fault

- ask forgiveness for your percentage of fault

People who fail to be accountable and responsible assume a selfish, victim mentality that escalates conflict.

Wise people want to be held accountable for their choices.

(See Figure 22)

0% My Responsibility	Your Responsibility 100%
My Admission	Your Admission
My Resolution	Your Resolution
My Apology	Your Apology
My Forgiveness	Your Forgiveness

Figure 22

THE LAW OF PERSPECTIVE

Truth is not always from your perspective. Events are not always as they appear to you. We don't know what we don't know.

Most conflicts have two perspectives—some truth and some error may exist in both perspectives.

Being "right" from your perspective may not be "right" from another person's perspective.

Be cautious about acting forcefully or aggressively only from your perspective. Learn to weigh data—and your own perspective.

Perspective enlarges with wisdom, knowledge, and understanding.

Even though your perspective may be "right," your response may be wrong if it results in a fractured relationship.

THE LAW OF PLACES

Our place in life (where we live) affects who we become in life.

"Location—location—location!" is the golden rule for real estate sales—but not necessarily for people.

Toxic places hurt people. Healthy places improve people.

Leaving one place just to get away from where you are is not necessarily a solution to your hurts, frustrations and friends; they usually follow you!

We choose the places our minds visit. Virtues and principles guide our minds to right places—and right choices.

Don't be in the wrong place at the wrong time.

A place is usually where people affect us, and we affect them.

People who follow noble dreams usually live in noble places.

Bloom where you are. You can make "your place" a better place by being a better person than the people in your place.

People whose priorities are in the right place usually end up in the right place.

THE LAW OF PREPARATION

People who prepare to reach a goal usually do.

People who aim at nothing usually hit it.

Most people live in defeat and frustration because they fail to take definite steps of preparation to reach a goal.

When the going gets tough, the tough get going—toward somewhere.

Mature people have a goal (dream) and prepare to reach it.

Preparation requires sacrifice of preferences in place of necessities.

Preparation includes:

- selective eating
- training
- avoiding temptations
- purpose
- optimistic thinking
- work

Prepare today, play tomorrow. Play today, suffer tomorrow.

A purpose-driven life always operates with preparation today to reach a dream or goal tomorrow.

Rewards (raise, promotion, achievement) are the result of preparation, work, sacrifice, and a sense of purpose.

You are being prepared for the future by your choices of:

- friends
- priorities
- activities
- thoughts.

THE LAW OF PRETENDING

Pretending is the first stage toward a successful life purpose.

Children pretend to be adult heroes in order to play out fantasy and dreams as firemen, cowboys, policemen, doctors, soldiers, nurses, veterinarians, etc.

Pretending is merely visualizing a dream, a goal, a life purpose.

Without a vision (pretending) people fail to reach goals or have life purposes.

People who succeed at reaching life goals are people who first dreamed (pretended in their minds) of achieving the goal.

"People become successful by dressing, talking, walking, acting (pretending) as if they had already achieved their goals."—Lt. Col. Jim Lathrop

They "walk out" (live) (pretend) they are already successful—and they eventually are!

THE LAW OF
PREVENTATIVE DECISIONS

We prevent negative consequences while enhancing positive consequences by making wise decisions. We can prevent negative things from happening over and over to us by making a decision not to do whatever we do that hurts us again and again.

When tempted to repeat or do an act that clutters our mind and conscience, or damages our body, we can make a conscious mental decision to prevent that event, act or relationship from happening.

We yield to temptation because we do not detect the signals leading up to a negative experience, or we presume that we are an exception to negative consequences.

Some people erroneously think:

- "God is asleep when I act..."

- "I will not get caught..."

- "Everybody else is doing it..."

- "I am the exception..."

We give in to temptation at the level at which we focus our energy:

- Character
- Virtues
- Relationships
- Intellect
- Sex drive
- Goals

People whose thoughts and motives are noble avoid temptations to act at sensual or lustful levels that keep people victims of their own desires.

Most people are driven by "body focus," thus, most people live by drives and lust related to physical temptations.

Marriages fail because most people do not make relationship decisions at the love (spirit) level. Lust wears out in time. Love endures and grows as people make mental decisions to focus higher than at the lust level.

The ability to make good decisions is based at the spiritual level—virtues, love, principles, and values. Temptations can be avoided only as we call to mind and apply virtues, principles and values at the spirit level at the moment of temptation. Virtue and chastity provide the best escape from sensual temptations.

At every temptation, your mind will pull you toward whatever you have purposed in your mind to be; a person of virtue or a person ruled by the appetites and desires of the body.

(See Figure 23)

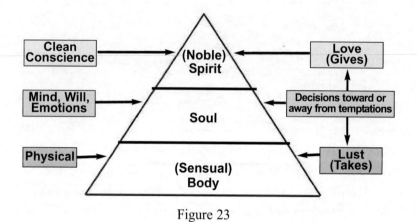

Figure 23

THE LAW OF PRINCIPLES

Our principles guide us because they form our core belief system by which we make choices.

People guided by virtues and moral principles are more secure and stable than people who make choices based on peer pressure, opinion polls, or popular practices.

A core set of values and principles stabilizes us with a base value system to pull us back to reality when we stray (negatives), enabling us to broaden our borders (positives) when doors of opportunity open.

Every choice (temptation or opportunity) is measured against our core value system (principles).

We should expect to become the kind of person reflected in our life principles. Our principles guide/direct our choices.

(See Figure 24)

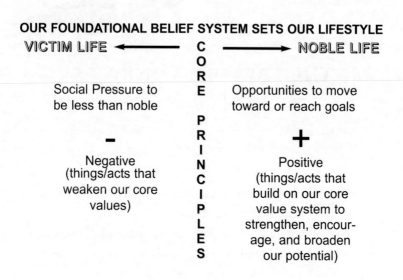

Figure 24

THE LAW OF PROBLEMS

Everyone has problems; some are worse than yours.

Wise people deal with them effectively; careless people let or cause problems to grow.

Someone said, "The world would be a great place to live if I didn't have to get along with people."

Life's problems are with self, environment, people, animals, or God—sometimes separately or in combinations.

Problems are the result or consequence of our own choices or the choices (lifestyle) of those in authority over us (man and God).

Problems can be our challenge to improve our position or circumstances in life or our excuse to remain a victim of our problems.

Mature people perceive problems as opportunities to apply character, energy, and training to "move on in life."

People who live by a moral code of ethics and values more easily solve or face problems.

Problems have to be faced and solved through a process, or they lead to more negative circumstances:

- *Face The Problem Maturely.*

- *Analyze It For Cause And Effect.*

- *Get Help To Understand & Face It.*

THE LAW OF PURCHASES

Purchases are for food, facilities, vehicles, investments, or fun.

People purchase items or services with cash, money orders, or debit cards (NOW), or with a written promise to PAY LATER, with a check or credit card.

Receipts are written/printed proof of purchase; receipts are retained (kept safe) for tax purposes, refunds/exchanges, and a record of spending habits.

A check is a written note from you to your banker, authorizing him to take (withdraw) money from your bank account to pay a merchant or service provider to whom you write the check. You write checks as long as you have money in your bank account. The bank sends you a monthly letter/report of the checks you have written and the balance (money) in your account. You pay a fee (penalty) for checks written when your account does not contain sufficient funds.

A credit card is a plastic note (communication) from you to your banker, authorizing him to loan you money to pay for merchandise or services. Your banker (VISA, Master Card, Discover Card, Shell Oil, J.C. Penny, etc.) sends a monthly letter/report demanding payment for the loan to you. You pay the loan (credit card invoice) by check or debit card on your bank account. Your credit card banker will charge up to 29% interest on loans which you fail to pay in full each month.

A debit card (ATM) is a plastic "key" that allows you (or anyone who has your card) to withdraw cash or to pay for purchases directly from your personal bank checking account, in which you previously deposited money from your pay check. Note: anyone who has access to your debit card can empty your bank checking account!

Direct Deposit is an arrangement by which your employer or other person deposits your paycheck or payment owed to you electronically directly into your personal bank account.

A loan is an advance of cash (money) from a bank or financial lending agency for a specific period of time. You pay interest fees of 4%-29% on the money you borrow (to purchase clothes, food, housing, transportation, education, etc.).

Your credit rating is your reputation for paying debts (credit cards, loans, checks). A poor credit rating will limit your ability to borrow money.

Debt is the money you owe for purchases made with a promise to pay later (credit cards, loans, charge accounts, etc.). Debt is the result of unwise or uncontrollable expenses. Wise people stay out of debt! A person in debt is a slave to his banker. Debt limits life choices and privileges. Debt is stressful and depressing. Most credit card debt is for pleasure (restaurants, movies, designer clothes, new furniture, habits, etc.) rather than essentials.

To Cosign means to guarantee payment of another person's debt. Wise people do not cosign for other people, because their default on payment obligates the cosigner to pay the debt in full.

THE LAW OF
PUTTING OFF UNTIL
TOMORROW

Circumstances operative today will likely escalate to be faced tomorrow unless confronted in some definitive recovery plan today.

People who operate in a victim mentality seldom change their tomorrow; they keep repeating today's circumstances while blaming other people or conditions.

Recovery begins with acknowledgement of existing circumstances, avoiding a victim mentality, and assumption of responsibility to look for solutions.

The time to get past your past is today; otherwise, tomorrow will be a repeat of today.

Successful men are those who begin work on tomorrow's goals today.

Before retiring for bed (or leaving your work place), list the tasks, goals, or responsibilities to be completed tomorrow.

Plan today what you intend to do tomorrow.

Wise people frequently glance back to yesterday to measure achievement against success today, then peek toward tomorrow to plan for it.

THE LAW OF RESPONSIBILITY AND PRIVILEGES

Privileges are the product of assumed responsibility (the maturation process). The more responsibility we practice as a youth, the more privileges we experience in adulthood.

Privileges increase with assumed responsibility for such acts as punctuality, thoroughness, commitment, diligence, obedience.

Assumed responsibility earns:

- Praise from authority

- Greater responsibility

- Affirmation of your goals or life purpose

- Options to problems

(See Figure 25)

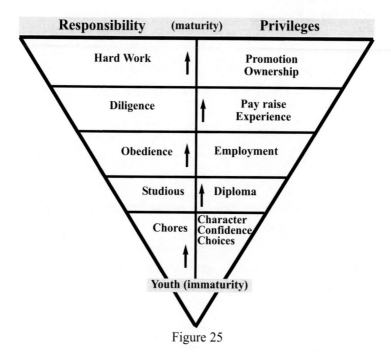

Figure 25

THE LAW OF SAFETY
(IN THE FACE OF FEAR)

A safe environment releases the ability to trust people and pursue goals.

A safe setting enables a traumatized teen to act in trust rather than to apply his/her survival tactics or instincts to overcome fear by fighting, stealing, lying, or arguing.

Trust is an open door to success.

Bonding with a trustworthy mentor is possible where the teen feels safe.

Toxic thoughts diminish in safe environments.

Fear stifles creativity and achievement; it strangles positive thinking.

The best way to overcome fear is to position yourself under the watch-care of a noble person who can protect you and guide your life choices and thoughts.

Fear can be a catalyst (motivation) to pursue a new lifestyle (to be a different kind of person than the people who created your fear).

Running with the wrong crowd increases the probability of fear (of consequences).

Hanging with the right people reduces the likelihood of fear of consequences.

People who feel safe release creativity and energy to soar with eagles.

Wise life choices improve safety.

THE LAW OF SEEDS

We harvest crops from seeds (acts) we sow.

We are impacted by the harvest around us.

Words are seeds (spoken or received).

Acts are seeds (done or experienced).

Seeds which are weeds (greed, hate, anger, lust, bitterness) will reproduce in like kind unless starved of nutrition.

Thought-seeds (positive or negative) become acts if allowed to grow.

As a man thinks, so is he.

Bring every negative thought into captivity (control) immediately or it will be cultivated by toxic lifestyle habits, customs, associates, traditions, and desires.

Out of the heart (thought chamber) comes the seeds/ choices of life.

The thought-seeds we allow to be cultivated will determine the life-crop we harvest.

Sow a thought, reap an act; sow an act, reap a habit; sow a habit, reap a destiny.

A soul filled with toxic thought seeds can be cleansed by replacing the toxic seeds with the good seed of virtue, kindness, goodness, chastity, grace, mercy, love, and truth.

THE LAW OF SELF-DISCIPLINE

A person who cannot say "NO" to temptations will say "YES" to whatever appeals to immediate impulses, desires, lusts, threats, fears ...

Success is measured over time and is the result of self-discipline of body, soul and spirit to reach defined goals (dreams). Wise people develop moral character to resist immediate temptations, and practice self-discipline in eating, relationships, experiences, exercise, thought, rest ... etc.

Goal attainment and self-discipline are co-dependent. Self-discipline says "NO" to any thing, act, or person which could weaken goal attainment for self or another person. You can more easily walk away from temptation when focused on a lofty or noble cause.

Learn to say "NO" to temptation.

THE LAW OF SERVICE

Meeting the needs of others through service meets our needs for life purpose.

Discovery of our life purpose is the result of an external source which serves us.

While we serve others, we pour out and replenish some of our own resources, keeping us energized by life purpose.

People who live with focus on themselves fail to find life purpose.

Heroes are people who respond to the need of others in times of peril or danger.

Service may be seasonal or a lifetime:

- singing, illustrating, parenting, ranching/farming, construction work, writing, managing, operating, nursing, accounting, engineering, cooking/baking, protecting, teaching, training, broadcasting, preaching, mowing/landscaping, plumbing, inventing, building, tailoring/sewing, manufacturing, transporting, interpreting, inspecting, surveying, etc.

Effective service is manifested through our gifting, temperament, talent, skill, and training.

THE LAW OF SEX

The word "Sex" has three meanings:

- Gender (male or female)
- Act of marriage between husband and wife
- Act of lust between two people

Sex is based on one of two motives:

- Love (mature) (restraint before marriage)
- Lust (immature) (selfish hunger for sensual pleasure)

The object of our thoughts/virtues determines whether sex is based on lust or love.

Love is based on spiritual, physical, and emotional (body, soul, spirit) values. Lust never satisfies. Lust leaves a person's needs unfulfilled and unsatisfied with an empty feeling.

The act of sex in marriage is approved by the Creator (God-initiated). Sex is fully understood and relevant only when exercised as intended between a husband and wife. Sexual acts as entertainment outside of marriage are never fulfilling.

The sexual act between couples outside of marriage gathers negative memories which will forever be shared by future partners (husband/wife).

The desire and curiosity for sex is natural. It is a created drive.

When and with whom sexual desire is expressed is a matter of moral character, virtue, and chastity.

Sexual pleasure between a married man and woman is necessary for continuation of civilization.

Sexual expression between unmarried partners is merely lust (desire for sensual pleasure) and has negative consequences (HIV, STD's, cluttered conscience, fatherless children, poverty for mother/children).

Abstinence before marriage and faithfulness in marriage is the ONLY moral expression of sexual desire.

Lust IS NOT LOVE. Lust takes and abuses. Love gives. Every sexual partner becomes a permanent resident in the soul, body and spirit forever "shared" with the eventual spouse.

Males want to "conquer" and thus abuse sex. Girls want to "capture" and thus sacrifice purity and virtue when under the influence of romantic "I Love You" conversation (promises of security or pleasure).

Men are stimulated by touch and exposure to female flesh between the clavicle and the knees. Men presume that a girl who shows cleavage, bare back, hips, and mid section is advertising for and soliciting sexual attention, thus males press for and seek "favors" from such a girl.

Women dress "barely" to attract and capture male attention, not necessarily to "have sex," but to confirm womanhood. Men seek to "confirm" the girls' womanhood through sexual relationships or encounters before marriage.

Passion is natural. It happens when lust or love finds opportunity for expression (as in a secluded place). Thus, wise single people never get in a place or relationship where passion could find expression in the "act of marriage."

The greatest gift a person can give in a marriage is sexual purity. Where and when the "act of marriage" is expressed is a matter of moral courage, maturity and perspective of reality. The most effective defense against abuse of "the act of marriage" is involvement in and commitment to a noble lifestyle—a purpose-driven life that channels energy (body, soul, spirit) toward fulfillment of a worthy goal for both partners. A person is ruled by whatever is allowed to capture passion.

People of moral courage keep desire for sex under control and in perspective at moments of temptation.

A noble person never abuses another person who is hungry for love or acceptance.

THE LAW OF THE "S" FACTORS

Some things in life are beyond your control to change, but hope increases when you apply the "S" factors to change negative conditions within your control:

1. Speak kindly and respectfully with others

2. Sleep well (7–8 hours daily) with a clear conscience

3. Stop griping and grumbling about your situation

4. Study diligently toward a good goal

5. Stay focused on daily duties

6. Surround your life/thoughts with positive people, music, literature, and media

7. Swallow real food … rather than junk food

8. Seclude yourself regularly to meditate on wisdom

9. Seek wise counsel from people of integrity

10. Shun people who do not bring out your best qualities

11. Strengthen your body with exercise.

THE LAW OF
SITUATIONAL AWARENESS

"Stay in the moment"—be aware of what is going on around you and be prepared to avoid danger and seize opportunities to fulfill your vision.

We usually do wrong because we fail to avoid people, places, and situations where "bad" is about to happen.

Wise people "create" good situations by selecting the right people with whom to associate, the right places to be in and the right principles to obey. When guided by virtue and principles, we detect the situations around us in time to evade negative consequences. Wise people place themselves in situations where good things can happen.

The safest place to be is away from unsafe places. Stay away from situations, places, and people where bad things happen; don't go there!

THE LAW OF SLEEP

Sleep is required for the body, soul, and spirit to perform as designed.

Without adequate sleep, people are grumpy, easily irritated, less efficient, less healthy, and possibly dangerous to self and others.

The average person needs about eight hours of uninterrupted sleep nightly.

A clear conscience toward self, others, and God is the best formula for sleep.

Sleep is enhanced by eating the evening meal before 7 p.m. and engaging in relaxing conversation, or reading/memorizing inspirational material at least fifteen minutes prior to bed time.

Sleep is "stolen" by engaging in or observing anger, bitterness, strife, pornography, grief or abusive behavior (toward or by other people).

Sleep is better after a shower/bath, clean and comfortable garments, and laundered sheets.

Speak, write, or do something kind, noble or encouraging to someone prior to retiring for the evening.

Express gratitude for at least three things, people, or circumstances before drifting off to sleep.

THE LAW OF SMALL STEPS

A long journey begins with the first small step in the right direction.

Turn your thoughts toward the goal (dream, aspiration, purpose).

Take *one small step* toward your noble goal, dream, or life purpose *today*.

Step away from distractive people, places or activities that could hurt you physically, emotionally, spiritually and deter you from reaching a positive goal.

Plan to succeed by finishing small steps one at a time.

Let other people help you identify little things that hurt your plan to succeed, and let them help you identify little things that will cause you to succeed.

Use each step (achieved) as a new foundation from which to take the next step toward your dream.

Each positive step encourages us to continue moving in the direction of our dreams.

Big achievements usually begin with one small step toward a dream.

THE LAW OF A SOFT ANSWER

A soft answer deflects wrath and disarms anger.

Agree appropriately with an angry person regarding faults. Then, ask questions to detect motives, gain perspective, or identify frustrations.

Acknowledge the proper authority status of the involved parties. If you are in the position of authority, you do not need to prove it. If you are under authority, you need to maintain a position of grace, rational behavior, and meekness.

Avoid provoking anger or hostility by maintaining your appropriate position in the hierarchy of authority by friendly posture, facial expressions, soft words, and control of emotions.

Appeal to conscience as applicable. Make an appeal to authority as applicable to reach your dream or fulfill responsibilities.

Acknowledge your faults and apologize as appropriate.

THE LAW OF SORROW

Sorrow breaks open our emotion (soul) to allow entrance of new insight about ourselves and others.

No one is exempt from sorrow. Everyone has tear ducts.

Sadness has the potential to make us better or bitter—depending on how we respond.

Hope is always the brother of sorrow/sadness. Hope deferred makes the heart sad.

Sorrow often is sister to anguish of soul which cries out, "Oh, God, Why Me?"

Sorrow is often the catalyst (force) that propels us out of mediocrity into greatness.

Sorrow passes quickly when we let it do its work to fix us.

THE LAW OF STRESS

Stress is the number one cause of illness (depression, physical health).

Stress is based on or related to:

1. Lack of forgiveness of/or bitterness toward another person

2. Grumbling, griping and fault-finding about circumstances

3. Anger toward a person or God

4. Association with negative peers or family

5. Negative or selfish desires and thoughts

6. Junk diet ("dead food")

7. Grief.

Stress can be relieved through attaining a healthy body, soul, and spirit. These can help:

1. Gratitude expressed for little things in life

2. Laughter at wholesome experiences

3. Service to others

4. Clean and virtuous thoughts, acts and conversation

5. Nutritious food—appropriate body weight

6. Living up to our national motto "In God We Trust"

7. Soaring with "eagles" who live above struggles

8. Daily physical exercise

9. Forgiveness against people who are or have been abusive.

Stress is the result of the way our brain (memories) and character process new information through mental toxic waste accumulated from participation in such things as pornography, occult practices, immoral or abusive sexual behavior, assault against others, selfish ambition.

A history of stored up emotional toxic waste (stressors stored in the mind) becomes the well from which the mind draws thoughts with which to handle new stressors.

Accumulated emotional waste encourages fear, depression, and more stress.

New thoughts based on love, hope, gratitude, forgiveness, virtues, and integrity will dilute or neutralize the threat of fear and the potential impact of stressors.

An effective way to reduce fear and stress is to renew the mind—to wash out the toxic waste build-up of past negative stressors with learning/memorization of new concepts, virtues, precepts, laws and principles that are stronger than the old "junk stressors" stored in the mind. Unaddressed stress leads to a life of depression and fear.

Stress replaced with positive virtues leads to hope, love, healing, and purpose. A new supply of virtues, wisdom, character, and knowledge equips the renewed mind to respond to stressors logically rather than emotionally.

Logical assessment of potential stressors allows a person to take control of the thoughts that will solve the problem (stressor).

Being labeled as bipolar may really mean that the brain has not developed the courage, character, and virtues necessary for identifying potential stressors and taking mental control of them before they "kick in" the emotions of fear and depression (which short-circuit the brain).

A past traumatic event (or series of events) may be the "toxic waste seed" that was allowed to grow as a major stressor. That past, emotionally-loaded toxic memory must be conquered through the act of forgiveness before the victim can begin to build a new well of positive memories from which to handle stressors.

THE LAW OF STRUGGLES

Struggles bring out our best qualities and help us discover latent talents and gifts we didn't know were part of us.

Critics and opponents force us to face weaknesses that if not conquered can lead to our downfall or acceptance of mediocrity.

Competition against champions makes us one.

Diamonds are shaped by abrasives.

Gold is refined by fire.

Struggles force us to persevere.

Perseverance accesses fulfillment.

Eagles live among high, rugged cliffs and learn to use (rather than struggle against) strong wind currents.

THE LAW OF SUPERSTITION

People who are superstitious are admitting that a "force" other than God and greater than mankind operates "at will" on the earth.

All cultures (groups of people) hold beliefs in the supernatural. Those beliefs are expressed in either superstition or a set of religious practices.

Superstition is based on fear that harmful results will occur if certain charms are not worn or if certain acts are done.

For example, superstitious people may try to appease the "force" by wearing such charms as a rabbit's foot, medallion, cross, skull, or some other fetish (symbol) under the false assumption that the "force" will be charmed or restrained from hurting the person (charmer). However, note that the display of a particular religious symbol is not necessarily indication of superstition, but may be simple acknowledgement or allegiance to a particular belief system.

Superstitious people may try to prevent "bad luck" (hurtful acts by the "force") by avoiding certain actions such as:

1. not stepping on a sidewalk crack;

2. not walking under a ladder;

3. taking an alternate route when a black cat crosses the path ahead;

4. avoiding the number 13 (hotel room, seat, row).

A famous teacher once told his audience, "I perceive that in all things you are too superstitious" because the people used statues, fetishes, and charms to appease idols and false gods. The teacher observed that superstition was an expression of fear that the world was under the influence of an evil force that could damage man's circumstances or fortune.

To act with superstition is to think about and admit the existence of a "bad god" to whom you are a servant. As you think about a "bad god," you will fear it, and in fact, worship it. You become like that which you fear or worship.

Wise people study the God of our forefathers and worship that which is lovely, kind, good, true, just, honest, and virtuous. They avoid worshipping any force which is based on harm, greed, sedition, strife, lust, seduction, theft, abuse, or superstition.

America's founding fathers observed that immigrants from throughout Europe, who settled in the colonies, practiced their beliefs and superstitions. Thus, when the Declaration of Independence and the U.S. Constitution were ratified, the founding fathers made a bold statement of their trust in God. Our national motto, "In God We

Trust," which first appeared in a poem by Francis Scott Key in 1812 later became the American national anthem. America's patriots knew in whom they believed and established a national practice of trusting God rather than practicing superstition about a "bad force."

THE LAW OF
SUSTAINED CHOICES

People continue to exercise lifestyle choices until confronted by authority and/or with alternatives which are perceived to be more rewarding than current practices.

Recovery efforts require counselors to persuade clients to choose an alternative practice that holds the promise (hope) of a more fulfilling lifestyle.

Persuasion to change lifestyle can occur through:

A. INTERNAL ACTION

1. Self assessment (take a good look at who you are)

2. Repentance (recognize your faults and turn from them)

3. Realization (identify your qualities and put them into action)

B. EXTERNAL ACTION

1. Restriction of choices/freedom to choose

2. Punishment/discipline/confinement (negative reinforcement)

3. Rewards/incentives (positive reinforcement)

4. Shame (public exposure of acts) (fear of public ridicule)

5. Appeal to conscience prompted via:

   a) Print (read good stuff that makes you better)

   b) Media (refuse to watch bad stuff that drains your character)

   c) Face-to-face dialog (run with good guys; don't walk or sit with losers).

People find happiness where life choices result in noble acts.

We are the result of our sustained choices.

THE LAW OF TABLE MANNERS

Proper table manners can establish or harm relationships.

Wise people learn how to eat properly:

— which fork to select for salad (outside edge)

— which knife to select for butter (round tip)

— which spoon to select for soup (round)

— which cup or glass to select for beverages (on your right)

— where to place the napkin (lap)

— how to hold the fork, spoon, knife (thumb & finger)

— how to summon a waiter (waitress) (hand motion)

— when to begin eating (after host begins)

— when to begin dessert (after others finish meal)

— when to speak during a meal (without food in mouth)

— when/how to place an order from a menu (follow host)

— how to choose a meal from the menu if you are

unfamiliar with the food choices or restaurant (ask waiter for suggestions)

— how much money to spend in accordance with your eating partners (whether you are the guest or the host). (follow lead of host)

How you hold a spoon or fork in a public place could affect your career.

THE LAW OF THINKING

Whatever feeds the mind shapes it.

As a person thinks, so is he or she.

Thoughts move people toward specific actions, temptations, habits, and goals.

Every act begins as a thought.

Thoughts exercised repeatedly form habit.

Habit determines character, and character guides thoughts.

Negative thoughts are neutralized or replaced only by positive thoughts which move the soul away from current toxic thought patterns.

People think well only when thoughts are focused on noble or lofty (eagle-like) goals.

The contents of the tank (well) from which thoughts are drawn determine the kind of acts we experience.

We think according to the data, virtues, values, and morals stored in the well of our soul (mind, will, emotions).

"Stinking thinking" leads to stinky consequences.

You are like the people who think like you think.

Think well, and you will act well.

Think about what you think about.

If you don't like what is happening in your life, think of a better lifestyle—and pursue it!

THE LAW OF
TODAY AND TOMORROW

We will be tomorrow the person we are today until we move away from our past relationships, habits, choices, abuses, and lifestyle that have shaped us.

If we keep doing (being) what we have always done, we will always be what we already are.

We are the cumulative result of our past decisions and experiences. They tend to control our thoughts and energy.

We don't know what we don't know about life choices and consequences. That's why we need to find new things on which to think.

In order to move away from the past, we need new information (knowledge) and experiences unlike those of the past.

Our future is determined by our character to change our present lifestyle.

Tomorrow will likely be no different than today unless you change something about your life today.

Today's thoughts about a noble tomorrow pull us from our past.

Who you are tomorrow is tied to who you choose to be today.

THE LAW OF TOO BIG

Don't be too big to do little things (without being asked), like:

- Change the toilet paper when the roll is empty

- Pick up scraps of paper or trash on the floor or sidewalk

- Pick a wildflower for a widow or orphan

- Write a note of appreciation or encouragement to someone having a rough day

- Start a conversation with a stranger who looks like he/she needs a friend

- Open the door for an elderly person, child, or someone whose hands are full

- Make your bed, hang up your clothes, straighten your shoes

- Wash the bathtub or shower, or clean the dishes

Little things can make a big difference.

THE LAW OF TOUGH LOVE

True love is giving a person what he/she needs without expecting personal benefits or privileges in return. (Love is not giving someone whatever he/she wants.)

Love is sometimes expressed through instruction, correction, reproof, and/or discipline.

Love requires helping a person realize/experience the consequences of choices while the person still has opportunity to adjust his/her lifestyle.

Sometimes love is to put a person temporarily where he thinks he doesn't want to be so he can eventually get what he needs/wants in life.

Successful people are those who experience the benefits of love expressed by people who were sometimes tough enough to say "NO" and wise enough to say "YES" to life choices.

THE LAW OF TRAUMA

A traumatic experience affects growth and function of your body, soul and spirit.

- Your body is hurt (traumatized) by mercury, lead, fluoride, diet, amputation, drugs, physical abuse or injury;

- Your soul (mind, will, emotions,) is damaged by loss of loved one, assault, abusive sexual experiences, abandonment, physical or emotional isolation, neglect, pre/post birth rejection, lack of bonding;

- Your spirit is weakened by exposure to occult practices, violence, pornography, premarital sex, absence of virtues and principles.

Trauma can "freeze" the soul (mind, will, emotions) at the moment in time of a traumatic encounter or experience causing "arrested development" of the mind, will, and emotions.

Adolescents may drift or be drawn emotionally toward the same type of traumatic experience (sexual assault, drugs, pornography, occult, gangs) which occurred years previously as a subconscious effort to find release from the "freeze" moment (traumatic event) that causes emotional torment.

The following symptoms may manifest at the "freeze point" of trauma: biting, bed wetting, tantrums, depression, dysfunctional speech patterns, restricted mental focus, cluttered or faulty reasoning, cognitive disabilities, promiscuity, obesity, undernourishment, anger, rebellion, grief, prejudice, hate. Drugs (prescription or illegal) can mask or suppress and/or can accentuate or exacerbate symptoms, but do not cure emotional pain or damage from abuse, poor choices or neglect by peers or adults.

Drugs interrupt and rechannel or redirect chemical-electrical flow of thoughts, emotions, and stimulations in/through the brain. Negative side effects occur (irrational acts): depression, suicidal, mood swings, anxiety, weight instability, appetite changes, nightmares, hallucinations, fear, drives.

RELEASE ("thawing" of the freeze moment that arrested learning) is possible for the traumatized or toxic person:

- The Body can experience release through diet change, chelation, mineral intake, fasting, exercise, therapeutic massages;

- The Soul can discover release through inspirational music, positive role models, noble literature and activities;

- The Spirit can become free through forgiveness, bonding love, affirmation of worth, confession of guilt, forsaking toxic practices, meditating on virtuous concepts.

Realize that you are worth far more than the level of worth you have assumed for yourself based on the abuse or neglect to which you were subjected!

The way to get over anguish or pain from past experiences is to base your life choices on chastity, virtues, principles, and values that bring out the best qualities of you and the people with whom you associate ... and to be virtuous in all relationships.

THE LAW OF TRUST

A man who can be trusted will always be employable.

An untrustworthy man is as painful to an employer as a broken tooth and a sprained ankle.

A man feels confident when he knows he is trusted.

Trust is earned by doing what is expected without being watched by a boss, parent, teacher, or spouse.

"You can trust him," is one of life's highest compliments.

People who are trusted with little things (information, tasks, duty, money) will be trusted with bigger things (money, property, responsibilities, privileges).

Trust is a matter of character based on morals, virtues, and principles which govern decisions.

The test of a man's character is how well he can be trusted when tempted to live below a noble level.

A person controlled by sensual lust, pornography, greed, anger, substances, pride, bitterness, fear or jealousy is not trustworthy in critical circumstances or relationships.

A trustworthy person always protects the reputation, possessions and virtues of other people.

A person who says, "You can trust me," may not necessarily be trustworthy—Look at his/her character!

Trust is earned. It is a virtue. It is eagle-like!

THE LAW OF
UNCHANGEABLES

Some things never change; they have to be accepted as reality.

Unchangeables are often catalysts that influence and shape our destiny.

Some common unchangeables are skin color, ethnicity, family history, parentage, death, or loss of family members, past abuses, failures, or successes.

People who think they can or should change their unchangeable live in anxiety, fantasy, and failure.

People who accept their unchangeables with gratitude and appreciation as marks of identity tend to become successful.

People who accept their unchangeables as marks of distinction possess the qualities of world changers. They focus on what they can do to make the world a better place—they change changeable circumstances and laws, they provide hope, creativity, peace of mind, and inventions.

Night time is unchangeable (it occurs every day), but Thomas Edison invented the light bulb that changed the way the world functioned at night.

Human nature is predictably selfish, but Jesus of

Nazareth demonstrated a better way to live, and He changed the world. Humans can't fly by changing their arms into wings or by growing wings; however, the Wright brothers invented a machine that could fly and in which men could ride.

Gladys Aylward couldn't change World War II, but she did rescue hundreds of Chinese orphans who were victims of Japanese attacks.

Martin Luther King, Jr. and Rosa Parks could not change their ethnicity, but they did change the way they were treated in public places.

Abraham Lincoln couldn't change the fact that his mother died when Abe was a small boy, but Mr. Lincoln grew up to become world famous for turning unchangeable disappointments into opportunities.

THE LAW OF VALOR

Within every male is the natural instinct and drive to exercise valor. Valor is involvement in a noble cause, especially to defend widows, orphans, strangers, freedom, and virtue.

Valor is powered by virtue (moral character) and courage. Valor turns to selfish lust when influenced by greed, pride, or desire for power to rule people.

Valor maintains freedom; lust destroys the foundations of freedom.

Men are motivated by the nature of their character: virtuous and noble or greedy, selfish, and arrogant.

A man of valor protects the virtue of others, especially widows and the fatherless.

"Men of valor are trustworthy. Men of valor are courageous." (Ref: *Brave Heart*)

"Every noble cause has at its heart men of valor." (Ref: *The Patriot*)

THE LAW OF VIRTUE

Impact the world with virtue, rather than allow the world to impact your virtue.

Unwise decisions result in pain. Wise choices based on virtue produce hope, joy, and laughter.

Make no provision for the flesh (put aside opportunities to taint the soul).

Focus Courageously:

- Sight—things that strengthen virtue

- Sound—music that soothes the heart and mind by building virtue (goodness)

- Read—books and magazines that "refresh" the soul

- Places—experiences that sharpen perspective and values

- Friends/peers—associates who encourage you to be an eagle!

Virtue keeps you out of the ditches of regret, sorrow, and consequences—and on the road to your dreams.

THROUGH VIRTUE
Walls of bitterness
And
Towers of anger
FALL;

And in their place
Pillars of mercy
And
Monuments of grace
RISE!

THE LAW OF THE WARRIOR

In every man is the fantasy of being a noble warrior.

Every little boy imagines himself slaying enemy soldiers in defense of mothers and sisters.

In the souls of men is the warrior concept to defeat enemies and preserve freedom.

A man is at his best when defending a noble cause; he is at his worst when opposing goodness.

Because evil is a universal presence, every man has but to look around to find a noble cause in which to be a warrior.

THE LAW OF WHO YOU ARE

We are who we are.

We are *not* who others are.

We are *not* who others think we should be.

Every person is designed as a unique person with gifts (talents).

Secure people do not compete to be like (or better than) someone else.

We are becoming who we admire, emulate, or obey. Our temperament is our design—(sanguine, choleric, melancholy, phlegmatic)—which frames application of our strengths and gifts.

Unfulfilled and frustrated people are those who try to be someone else.

Be you—with virtue & moral character and you will be successful.

Your identity is in your design, gift, and sense of purpose. We fail in life when we try to find our identity in titles, achievements, events, people, possessions, and clothes.

We enjoy who we are when we walk daily in virtue, kindness, goodness, and purpose.

You are who/what you allow to shape your thoughts.

These things impact your body, soul, and spirit by entering the "gates" to your life (sight, smell, taste, touch, hearing):

- *Food* is usually toxic or nutritious;

- *Drugs* have side effects that affect body chemistry and function;

- *Images* stimulate virtuous or toxic thoughts and sensations;

- *Experiences* are the basis of trauma, achievements, conversion, affirmations;

- *Responses* are determined by forgiveness, bitterness, anger, envy, hate, joy.

Sometimes the best decisions involve no participation [Say, "No" to toxic thoughts, people, activities, media, and substances]. A major part of reaching your dream is to exercise moral courage to make deliberate, forceful decisions to select how, who, what, when, and where your life will be impacted—and that you will put yourself only in situations or relationships that increase your options to reach your dream!

(See Figure 26)

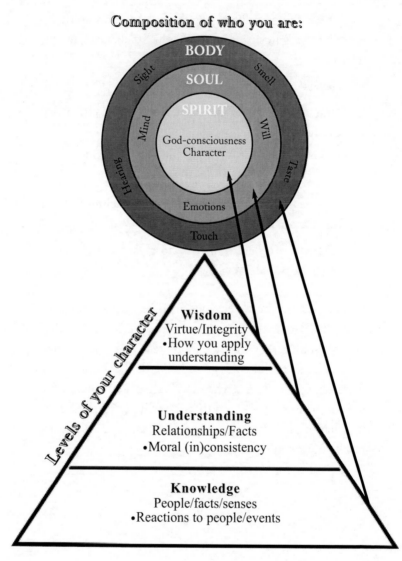

Figure 26

THE LAW OF
WILLINGNESS TO CHANGE

A person keeps a sense of life purpose only as he or she is willing to make adjustments in choices that align personal responsibilities and relationships with a noble goal.

Routine confrontations with people, obstacles and tasks (stressors) challenge our perspective about life, forcing us to make emotional or actual adjustments in our daily priorities.

Character and integrity determine how well we make adjustments in human relationships and career responsibilities.

People who reach noble goals constantly measure their own character and responsibilities against obstacles or people that "pop up" to delay, side-track, shut off, or accelerate plans for success.

Every material or financial obstacle, human confrontation, or unexpected intervention of our plans can be viewed as either an opportunity to mature or stress us to claim the status of a victim.

People who blame others for failure to reach goals are usually self-classified victims (…"of circumstances that were not my fault …"). Such people usually are not willing to accept responsibility for their own choices … they are unwilling to change their lifestyle. They look for other people or circumstances to blame so they can justify choices.

Every human is flawed; even the best people have a "human side" that is less than perfect. That side usually "shows up" when we are challenged in our quest to reach a goal.

Wise people recognize their humanness (flaws) and are willing to make adjustments to correct character weaknesses, mistakes, poor choices, lack of training, or immaturity. They learn to say, "Oops, I messed up; I'm sorry. Let me try again."

Successful people do not try to make themselves a victim of another person's action or flaws. Individuals who hope to succeed assume responsibility for their percentage of fault, and adjust their lifestyle to get back on focus to reach their dream or to fulfill their responsibilities.

(See Figure 27)

| Victim | 1 | 25 | 50 | 75 | 100 | Achiever |

How much was <u>really</u> my fault or responsibility? Success is to take full responsibility to reach your goal regardless of the actions of other people.

Figure 27

THE LAW OF THE WIND

Eagles catch wind currents to reach heights beyond the ability of other birds.

Eagles dare to fly where other birds dare not even try—for eagles are created to soar.

Wind can destroy or assist, depending on how it is avoided or harnessed for use.

Wind currents generally flow west to east around the world. Currents flow counter-clock wise to create storms that generate inclement weather patterns that distribute moisture and activate ions necessary to sustain the world's food chain.

Everyone faces necessary turbulence in life on a regular basis. "Eagle people" learn to catch the wind to soar with the turbulence.

Storms are opportunities to soar above circumstances—look for wind currents you can ride to heights above the turbulence around you.

You, like an eagle, are equipped to soar, but you must do as the eagle does—he catches a wind thermal that will take the eagle where other birds dare not (cannot) fly.

THE LAW OF WINNERS

People who win know where they are soaring; they have a goal!

Winners soar among companions who are also soaring!

Winners avoid the wrong crowd: eagles soar with eagles and avoid company of buzzards, turkeys and chickens!

Winners sacrifice personal desires in order to be well prepared for the race.

Winners focus thoughts on the race to be won; they push out of their minds any ideas, temptations or suggestions that would negatively affect focus on the race toward their dreams!

Winners don't quit; they rest, take a breath, and soar!

THE LAW OF WORDS

Words heard or spoken have power to shape life (self-image, confidence).

What you say is what you get (self-talk: affirming or debilitating).

Words of affirmation elevate a sense of noble worth. ["You are as noble as an eagle." "You are trustworthy."]

Words of condemnation denigrate to low self-esteem. ["He acts like a sneaky fox." "He is a vulture."]

Words sooth or inflame conflict.

Words express our thoughts, feelings, and emotions, and tend to determine how we act.

You have the choice to reject or accept words spoken to/about you.

Spoken or written words cannot be retracted.

Some words can only be "eaten."

Think before you speak or write words based on anger, hate, jealousy, lust, bitterness, or other unvirtuous qualities.

Let people say of you, "He/she always speaks kindly/honestly."

THE LAW OF WORK

Work is applied at jobs.

Work provides income for the worker and profit for the employer.

Work earns wages with which to purchase food, shelter, transportation, protection, recreation, and apparel, and to support ministries and charities, and to meet the needs of widows and orphans.

Work provides an opportunity to apply your temperament, gifts, training and talents in job responsibilities.

He who is able but who does not work should not eat!

Your paycheck is your reward for work that produces products or services that generate profits for your employer.

Work is taxable by local, state, and federal governments which take a percentage from your paycheck which has to be matched and/or paid by your employer before you receive your paycheck.

Paychecks increase as your work produces more products or services for your employer.

Job promotion is the result of hard work that makes you more valuable to your employer.

Every job is an opportunity to add skills and positive references to your resume.

Employers look for workers with lifestyles that reflect integrity, punctuality, honesty, character, dependability, diligence, and commitment to quality performance.

Work is labor + attitude + skill to earn money or complete projects.

People work in order to survive.

Work is energy invested in tasks or responsibilities that earn wages or results.

Work is a privilege - not a right.

Work (Labor) is of value to the employee (you) and employer (boss) only to the extent that your labor results in profit for the employer.

Good workers:

- Listen to or read instructions,

- Follow orders/instructions,

- Stay focused to responsibilities,

- Seek opportunities to learn,

- Do more than is expected,

- Report to the "boss" when tasks are completed.

Wages are the result of work.

Wages increase as the worker becomes more valuable to the employer's business.

Work is honorable if it is for a legitimate or noble cause.

People "get jobs" to earn money to pay for essentials

(food, clothing, shelter, transportation, education, etc.) or to purchase items for recreation, pleasure, entertainment, gifts, etc.).

A "job" should always be short term; wise "workers" stay (remain) employed in a "job" only long enough to gain skill, knowledge, understanding and wisdom to attain a dream!

There is no short cut to dreams. Every "job" is an opportunity to learn new insights about people, skills, responsibilities, and tools.

People who do not know how to work try to gain money by theft, begging, robbery, stealing, extortion, or selling illegal items (drugs, stolen property, people, self). Such people display a victim mentality. ("It's not my fault I can't get a job.")

THE LAW OF THE "Z'S"

Drowsiness affects most people sometime at school, work, or church.

The reasons for Z's is more than boredom or lack of a good night sleep; head nodding in public stems from any of the following:

1. *Inadequate sleep* the previous night;

2. *Impact of drugs* (prescription and illegal);

3. *Ingestion of sugar* (carbohydrate food that turns to sugar);

4. *Incidents* that cause depression (abuse by or to someone else);

5. *Internal* rest and peace of mind (diminished adrenaline);

6. *Inopportune* digestion and elimination for biological relief;

7. *Improvident boredom*/Lack of noble life purpose.

Here are some suggestions:

1. *Make sure you sleep* eight hours nightly;

2. *Eat a balanced diet* with fresh vegetables and fruit daily, especially in conjunction with meat or bread items;

3. *Avoid junk food*, especially for breakfast (no soda, donuts, candy, sugar-coated cereal), and quantities of meat late at night;

4. *Keep your body and conscience clean* by avoiding abusive activities.

5. *Get a Life.* Pour your soul into something noble.

CONCLUSION

Anyone who has counseled with father-challenged youth understands the heart-wrenching emotions of a person who struggles with the consequences of negative life choices. Sadly, thousands of teenagers are held in the selfish grip of anger, bitterness, grief, depression, sense of abandonment, selfishness, and lost hope. Often, these emotionally loaded feelings are the result of adults who failed to guide, protect or nurture youth along life's road. The result is that multitudes of young people struggle through life with little hope of relief from the negative consequences of their own choices or the lifestyle values of adults. Moreover, adults who are positioned to help redirect troubled youth (parents, teachers, pastors and counselors) search for just the right words to point youth toward a new beginning based on hope, high aspirations and a clear conscience.

Teaching Eagles To Soar was designed to provide the guidance and teaching which biological fathers ought to provide for their children. The nurturing father will find a wealth of ideas and principles to impart to his children as he teaches them to "soar" above peer pressure, disappointments, consequences, abuses, and failures. However, the high percentage of fatherless youth demands that substitute dads (role models, pastors, teachers and counselors) be equipped to identify root causes of negative life choices, then to provide solid guidance and instruction designed to provide a new source for making decisions and life choices. Paternal abdication necessitates availability of substitute fathers in the form of printed material such as found in *Teaching Eagles To Soar*.

The author was rewarded with multitudes of embraces and expressions of gratitude from youth who benefited from counseling sessions based on "Laws of Eagles" which became *Teaching Eagles To Soar*.

A seventeen year old daughter of a convicted felon said, "You saved my life."

An abandoned fourteen year old girl said, "Thank you for showing me that God cares for me. That gives me hope."

An eighteen year old boy of divorced parents said, "I never was taught anything like this by my father."

A stately teenage girl wiped tears as she admitted, "I wish my dad had taught me as you do; I could have avoided a lot of bad consequences."

A high school graduate said, "In college I will always be guided by your teaching."

A professional football player wept as he griped a copy of Teaching Eagles To Soar and said, "I never was taught how to live; I need this book!"

Such compliments can be cherished by other adults who decide to demonstrate "The Laws of Eagles" and to teach from this practical source. The author welcomes correspondence from persons who apply *Teaching Eagles To Soar*. (Learn@pacworks.com).

HOW TO INTERVIEW
A TEENAGER WITH 20 KEY
QUESTIONS

The purpose of the following questions is to build a positive relationship between the mentor and student. Each question is designed to "walk the student" through memories of his/her past life experiences (history) in an effort to discover where (if) trauma occurred that arrested learning and/or initiated bitterness, anger, grief, depression, a sense of hopelessness or low self-esteem.

It is essential that the student identify when, where and what life experiences occurred to "dampen" hope and cause toxic thoughts to dominate the student's mind, will and emotions such that school, home or placement facility became a burden to endure. This process is referred to as "emptying the glass." The intent is to identify the negative and toxic life style experiences that contributed to failure in school (and consequent anger, bitterness, depression, hopelessness, grief) so the counselor and/or parent can begin a rebuilding (refilling the glass) process based on positive qualities.

QUESTIONS TO ASK STUDENTS
AT INTERVIEWS OR
COUNSELING SESSIONS

1. Why do you want to attend this school or talk with me?

2. Are you below grade level in any subjects? (Have you failed any courses?) _____ Yes _____ No
What _____

3. Why did you fail? _____ Attendance _____ Attitude _____ Drugs_____ Relationship _____ Other _____

4. What do you need to do to make up the failed course (grade)? Tutorials? Complete assignments? Other:
_____

5. If you knew you could not fail, what career would you pursue? [What is your idea of the perfect career for you?]

6. What was the greatest experience of your life?

7. What was the most difficult or hurtful thing that has happened to you and/or your family?

8. If you could fix anything in your life or family what

would it be? _____

_____

9. Whom do you admire the most? Who do you want to be like?

10. Are you angry, resentful or disappointed toward anyone? Who? Why?

11. What thoughts or conditions need to change in order for you to graduate?

12. Can you name anything going on in your life that could prevent you from graduating?

13. Have you been: On probation? Suspended? Expelled? Arrested? If yes, Why? What have you changed in your life to avoid repeating the cause?

14. What are your daily responsibilities before and after school? _____
    Job _____ Ph # _____
    Employer's Name _____

15. Is there any reason why you can not arrive at school on time each day? _____

    a) Who will be dropping you off and picking you up at school? Name _____
       Their Phone # _____

    b) What kind of car _____
       color _____ License Plate # _____

16. Is there any reason why you cannot wear clean, wrinkle free and appropriate clothing as described in the Handbook?

17. Is there anything in the Student Handbook that will be difficult for you to obey?

18. Do you agree to honor the Handbook regarding: Body piercing ____Tattoos ____ Clothing ____ Phones ____ Attendance ____ Academics

19. Would you like to participate in service learning trips to other states or cities?

20. How can I help you reach your dreams?

ABOUT THE AUTHOR

Ronald E. Johnson has been a recognized voice in public and private education for more than 45 years. He is married to Nancy (Foster) Johnson. They have been happily married since their college days at the University of Arizona. Both majored in education. Dr. Johnson earned two post-graduate degrees (M.Ed. and Ed.S) at the University of Arizona and a C. Ph.D. from The International Institute. He was awarded an L.L.D. from Louisiana Baptist University.

Dr. Johnson is an author, seminar speaker and a certified public school administrator. He has conducted educational projects throughout the world. He was among the first Texas educational entrepreneurs to design and operate public contract and charter schools in Texas. He is the founder and president of Paradigm Accelerated Curriculum & System, which provides training and virtue-based, individualized learning textbooks used in private and public schools throughout North America and in numerous foreign countries.

The author grew up in a dysfunctional family with an abusive father. Both parents were violently murdered when Ronald was a teenager. His older brother was also murdered a few years later. Ronald "survived by grace" while taking jobs as forest ranger, clerk, and bookkeeper to help pay for college.

Teaching and administrative jobs in public and private schools provided experience that earned awards and respect. Dr. Johnson was a public school administrator before age 30. He was among the top 66 educators in America sponsored by the Ford Foundation and helped develop and administer a large textbook publishing company for 21 years. He was listed in Who's Who in Arizona Education. He has conducted seminars throughout North and Central America on virtue-based learning and father-challenged teenagers. Dr. Johnson was a featured guest on 60 Minutes, and USA Today recognized his Texas contract school among America's top 58 effective programs for recovering at-risk youth. The Center for Educational Reform listed the author among America's "Action Heroes" in recognition of his achievements in educational reform.

OTHER FAMILY BOOKLETS
BY DR. JOHNSON

How to Get a Grip on Parenting

Riddles from Science & History to Tease the Mind

Skateboards and Butterflies

Window in the Hill Country (Literature for Kuntry Kids)

Available at: www.pacworks.com